The Great Traits of Champions

Fundamentals for Achievers, Leaders, and Legacy Leavers

by

Mark Tewksbury

and

Debbie Muir

Best – great
success!

| GREAT | TRAITS | INC.

Library and Archives Canada Cataloguing in Publication

Tewksbury, Mark, 1968-
    The great traits of champions: fundamentals for achievers, leaders, and legacy leavers / Mark Tewksbury, Debbie Muir.

ISBN 978-0-9809083-0-5

1. Achievement motivation.   2. Success—Psychological aspects.
3. Leadership.   4. Self-actualization (Psychology).   5. Motivation
(Psychology).   I. Muir, Debbie, 1953- II. Title.

BF503.T47 2008   158.1   C2008-900148-6

Developed and Produced by Focus Strategic Communications Inc.

Project Management: Ron Edwards, Adrianna Edwards
Interior Design: Val Sanna
Interior Layout: Carol Magee
Developmental Edit: Ron Edwards
Copy Edit and Proofread: Linda Szostak

Cover Design by Emmanuel Bégin

www.thegreattraits.com

| GREAT | TRAITS | INC.

Table of Contents

Welcome to *The Great Traits of Champions*   1

The Achiever Traits: *Fundamentals for Being a Champion*   5
Introduction to Achiever Traits   6
Trait 1: Ask Yourself Questions   11
Trait 2: Expand Your Perspective   17
Trait 3: Make a Plan   23
Trait 4: Act Effectively   31
Trait 5: Go the Distance   37
Trait 6: Be Innovative   43
Trait 7: Utilize Power of Thought   49
Trait 8: Generate Enthusiasm   59
The Final Achievement: Becoming a Champion   64
Key Concept Synopsis   66
Achiever Traits—Self Assessment   67

The Leader Traits: *Creating Champion Organizations and Teams* 71
Introduction to Leader Traits   72
Trait 1: Be Aware   75
Trait 2: Have Purpose   83
Trait 3: Create Synergy   89
Trait 4: Show Conviction   99
Trait 5: Communicate Effectively   107
Trait 6: Exemplify Excellence   115
Trait 7: Embrace Contradictions   123
Trait 8: Continually Evolve   131
Key Concept Synopsis   138
Leader Traits—Self Assessment   139

The Legacy Traits: *Championing a Meaningful Way of Life*   143
Introduction to Legacy Traits   144
Trait 1: Embody Values   149
Trait 2: Challenge Convention   153
Trait 3: Influence Wisely   157
Trait 4: Have Humility   161
Trait 5: Show Goodwill   165
Trait 6: Celebrate Humanity   169
Trait 7: Live Now   173
Trait 8: Make Possible   177
Key Concept Synopsis   180
Legacy Traits—Self Assessment   181

Championing the Great Traits   183

Welcome to *The Great Traits of Champions*

Within these pages, we will take you on *The Champion's Journey*. For us, being a champion doesn't necessarily mean being number one. But it does mean not settling for mediocrity. Champions create an environment around them where excellence can thrive, and where great outcomes can happen. They stand up for what they believe in, and commit to making a positive impact with their lives.

We come from the world of sport. *Debbie Muir* is one of the Olympic movement's most winning coaches. She led her athletes to win seven out of a possible nine World Championship gold medals, as well as two Olympic gold and two Olympic silver medals in the sport of synchronized swimming. *Mark Tewksbury* is an Olympic champion, a three-time Olympic medalist, and seven-time world record holder in the sport of swimming. Combined, we have over 70 years of experience in becoming, producing, and being champions.

In sport, it is easy to relate to the idea of champions. It is part of the culture. But in fact, champions are found in all industries and domains. Business leaders are champions of commerce. Nobel Peace Prize winners are champions of humanity. Parents are champions of their kids. The point is that in some way, we are *all* champions in our lives. The important question is, do *you* see yourself that way? This book will show you how.

This Book Is a Guide to Being a Champion in Life

In sport, ideas like winning, coming out victorious, and being our best were ingrained into our psyche. Just as the world of sport demanded the best from us, so are many people being asked to constantly be better, to thrive within the competitive reality of a global marketplace, and to apply themselves more effectively in both their personal and professional lives. Unfortunately, most of us have never formally been taught the skills needed to meet these challenges in order to consistently perform at this level. Sometimes we hit the mark, other times not, but even when we do, it is hard to repeat because we are not exactly sure how we got the results that we did in the first place. This book will change that.

What lie ahead are three distinct sections to be explored one at a time, each one building on the champion theme from a different perspective. The first part of the book looks at The Achiever Traits, identifying the fundamentals needed to achieve whatever you desire. In this section, you determine your win. The second part outlines The Leader Traits, focusing on creating high-performing teams and champion organizations. Here, the outcome is winning results. The final section looks at The Legacy Traits, focusing on ways of being that leave a meaningful and positive impact on the world around you. It is about creating the lasting win.

In working with people from around the world, we have discovered that the fundamentals of achievement, leadership, and legacy don't ever really change—they are timeless and universal. Within this book, we have identified the core ideas necessary to build upon to reach your full potential as an achiever, leader, and legacy leaver. Where these ideas get personalized is in their application, depending on your specific desires for your personal and professional life. This is where you need to participate, to bring these traits to life.

At the end of the day, as wonderful as ideas are, if you can't apply them and watch them grow, then what is the point? That being said, we appreciate how busy your life already is. The last thing you need is to have another chore to do. That is why the ideas within each trait are concise and easy to integrate into what you are already doing. There are many anecdotes throughout this book to show you how we have applied these ideas; if you have time, enjoy them. But pay special attention to the shaded, colored, and bolded areas of the book. These encapsulate the essential ideas. Once the traits are stripped down to the core, it is the ability to *apply* the basic fundamental ideas step-by-step, action-by-action, over a sustained period of time that adds up to rewarding results for yourself and others. If these ideas are not practiced, they simply sit as words on paper.

In terms of process, there is no right or wrong way to read this book. We recommend that you treat it as if it were three books—one for each group of traits (Achievers, Leaders, and Legacy). Take your time so that the learning sticks. Each section has eight traits, with visual support and graphic icons to give you an anchor to the ideas. Following each section, a simple evaluation tool will help you in identifying which of the traits you are already utilizing, and which ones need more attention. If you are looking for some guidance on where to tackle the traits, start here.

You will find as you begin to know this book more intimately that different traits will come to the forefront as you tackle new challenges. In fact, whenever you find yourself facing a new obstacle, we suggest you refer back to *The Great Traits of Champions*. Use it to discover which specific trait you need to focus on, and by improving, will lead you forward. As you become more familiar with the traits, you will see that the right trait will start to find you as you need it.

As we noted earlier, in sport it is fairly easy to relate to becoming a champion—to determine your win—but in other areas of life, it is not so obvious. As a parent, a businessperson, a teacher, a communications expert, a volunteer, a member of a board, a coworker, or a community activist—whatever you might be doing, we might not look at our lives in these terms. But every day, within each of these worlds is the chance to be a champion. It just depends on how we see things. Remember, being a champion doesn't necessarily mean being number one. It is about excellence, personal betterment, and making a positive impact with your life—however you determine that to be. *The Great Traits of Champions* will help you move through the world with a new perspective. Let *The Champion's Journey* begin.

The Achiever Traits

Fundamentals for
Being a Champion

Each of the Achiever Traits has a graphic icon highlighted in green to help support the key ideas found within. In keeping with the fundamental theme of the book, the images are simple and straightforward.

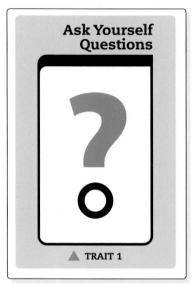

TRAIT 1:
The question mark gives us the green light to ask ourselves questions.

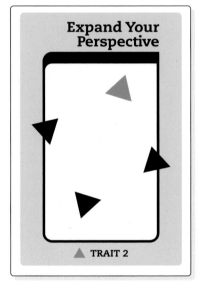

TRAIT 2:
The green arrow reminds us to look at things differently.

TRAIT 3:
The green star reflects the desired win that the plan leads toward.

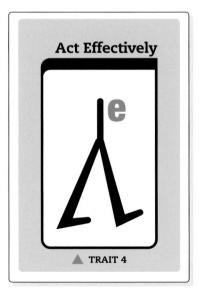

TRAIT 4:
A pair of walking legs with an "e" reminds us to GO forward "e"ffectively.

Use all eight icons as visual reminders of the key concepts and ideas found within each of the upcoming Achiever Traits.

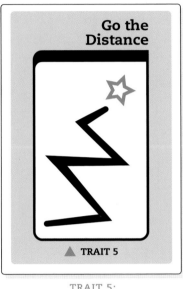

Go the Distance

▲ TRAIT 5

TRAIT 5:
The long, winding road leading to the green star represents enduring challenges.

Be Innovative

▲ TRAIT 6

TRAIT 6:
A blank slate represents innovation, making connections in new and creative ways.

Utilize Power of Thought

▲ TRAIT 7

TRAIT 7:
The thought bubble lifting a barbell reminds us to "work out" our mind.

Generate Enthusiasm

▲ TRAIT 8

TRAIT 8:
The beaming smile illustrates the infectiousness of attitude.

I N THE ACHIEVERS SECTION OF THIS BOOK, we look at eight fundamental traits that provide the rock-solid foundation from which any achievement can be built. Being a champion from this perspective means not settling for mediocrity and being the best at whatever you decide to do. This requires a process, and the simple ideas in this section outline a course of action that has proved time and again to act as a springboard to connect people to whatever they desire.

It is easy to fall into the trap of thinking that striving for excellence will make your life overly complicated, or that doing something extraordinary will be difficult. With this way of thinking, we can get overwhelmed before we even start. We have repeatedly found in working with people from all walks of life that in the pursuit of great things, we can sometimes forget about the simple things that actually work—this is why the traits in this book are called "Great"! By sticking to the basics within the following pages, and ensuring they are applied well and practiced consistently, you will build your capability and confidence knowing that through diligence and solid action, anything is possible.

Over the years, we have seen thousands of people use the ideas found in this section to reach many different objectives. In terms of being a champion, it doesn't matter what you decide that your win is. When we speak of winning, it does not mean that others lose. This is not necessarily about competing or comparing yourself to others. What we are trying to get across is that all of us have some kind of achievement that we desire to accomplish, and getting there is a win for ourselves. Whether it is being a top salesperson, being a great parent, giving an outstanding presentation, delivering a flawless musical performance, running a successful farm, or reaching a personal goal such as losing weight, the process to get to all of these personal wins remains the same.

We first used these traits when working together many years ago in the lead-up to the 1992 Olympic Games. For a year, we pursued an outrageous goal: Do what had previously taken seven years in less than one in order to become an Olympic champion. And we did it! This major achievement showed us firsthand that simple ideas followed through with action really do work.

At the beginning of each Achiever Trait, we will share a part of that Olympic story with you. What follows is a key concept that encapsulates the core learning, as well as simple steps and anecdotes that bring the main ideas to life. We conclude each trait with a Review that provides a summary and exercises to help you practice the trait. At the very end of the entire Achiever section is an evaluation tool. Use this tool to help you discover what your strengths and weaknesses are. As you read, you will most likely find that you have already mastered some of the Achiever Traits, but that others need more attention to consistently get the results you are looking for.

Your *Champion's Journey* begins here. The Achiever Traits are about thinking like a champion, acting like a champion, and ultimately being the champion in *your* life. Are you ready for the first trait?

ACHIEVERS

Ask Yourself
Questions

TRAIT 1

TRAIT 1:
Ask Yourself Questions

KEY CONCEPT
By becoming a master of the question, you stay connected
to yourself and to what you want to achieve.

DEBBIE: Our story begins at the Aquatic World Championships in Perth, Australia a year and a half before the Barcelona Olympics. I was coaching the synchronized swimming team, and almost every day Mark would come over and watch us practice. Although we had known each other in passing for many years, it was at this particular event that Mark and I started to become friends. Mark's 100-meter backstroke final was toward the end of the competition, close to when I was flying back to Canada, but I rearranged my schedule so that I could watch his race before going home. I was so glad I did. He swam one of the most exciting races I had ever seen.

MARK: *I had been on the national team for seven years, but this was my breakthrough. At the major international competitions in the past, I had always been fourth or fifth, which was certainly an achievement in its own right. But getting to the medal podium in my event had always eluded me. I was always just a fraction of a second off, which was heartbreaking. It was at these World Championships where I finally broke that cycle.*

11

DEBBIE: No kidding! You almost won the race. It was thrilling to watch because Mark was behind the entire time, but he never gave up. He kept coming back on the leader, and at the end of the race, he was only six one-hundredths of a second behind Jeff Rouse, the world record holder. With 18 months to go before the Olympics, Mark was finally on his way.

MARK: *Or so it had seemed. Fast-forward seven months to the Pan Pacific Championships in Edmonton, Alberta. I was competing against Jeff again, but this time it was in Canada so I had the hometown advantage. It would be the last time that Jeff and I would race each other before the Olympic Games the following year in Barcelona. My family and friends all traveled to watch the swim. The energy around the pool that night was electric. But instead of the come-from-behind victory I had envisioned, disaster struck.*

The noise was deafening as I finished the race. The crowd was going absolutely crazy. The problem was that I knew in my gut when I hit the wall that they were not cheering for me. I looked up to the scoreboard and found my name. My time—55:29—was exactly the same as I had posted in Perth. In the months since the World Championships, my strategy had been simple—don't change a thing. Amazing how well that works—don't change a thing, get the same result.

Above my name was Jeff's and his time—53:93. He had dropped 1.2 seconds off his Perth result and smashed the world record. To put that in perspective, when you added up all of my incremental improvements over the seven years I had been on the national team, it equaled 1.2 seconds. I now had less than 10 months to make the same gain if I had any chance of winning the Olympics. It didn't seem possible. I went from a fingernail away from my dream coming true to having to do the impossible. I was shocked, then depressed, then scared out of my mind.

So what had happened? Following my breakthrough swim at the World Championships, I had thought that I was really on the right track with what I was doing. When I went back to my day-to-day routine, I got a bit complacent. I didn't question how I might do things better, or even why I was doing them. In my mind, I had arrived, and I had started to take things for granted. The only thing I might have asked myself was how great it was going to feel when I inched ahead of Jeff by six one-hundredths of a second the next time we raced. Unfortunately, this hadn't been the right question.

In silence, I drove home from the competition, my head swirling with questions. I asked myself over and over, "What just happened? How did it happen? What am I doing?" I needed to regroup, to get clear, to give myself some time to honestly assess how things had turned out this way, and what I was going to do next.

BEING A CHAMPION MEANS:
1. Understanding the Power of the Question
2. Knowing What to Ask Yourself When
3. Being Honest with Your Answers

1. Understanding the Power of the Question

Asking questions helps us face the facts about where we find ourselves. Questioning connects us to reality. Sometimes that can be brutal, other times not. Regardless, it helps us find clarity, and allows us to consider the implications of what will happen if we continue to do the same things, or alternatively, what might happen if we do things differently. Questions help us find meaning and avoid complacency, and provide us with focus through the never-ending periphery of activity and distractions that we encounter daily. Such is the power of the question.

Keep in mind that all questions are not created equally. Different types of questions will lead you to different answers or outcomes. Soul-searching is an internal process that helps you feel more connected to yourself and what you are doing. These are questions like the following:

▲ *What* am I doing?
▲ *Why* am I doing it?
▲ What is *important* to me?

There is another type of question that is more external, focusing on where you find yourself with respect to the world around you. These are questions like the following:

▲ Where do I stand *in relation to* the best?
▲ What do I have to do *in order to* get there?
▲ What do I need to do *differently* or *keep doing*?

To maximize the power of the question is to master both sets of questions.

2. Knowing What to Ask Yourself When

Ask Yourself Questions is the first Achiever Trait because it is so fundamental to everything you do. As you make your way through this book, you will become more equipped to ask yourself better and better questions. Over time, you will know intuitively what kind of question to ask yourself, and when to ask it. We want you to start by noticing what kinds of questions you are asking yourself now.

Many of us don't take the time to stop and think about the *what, why, when,* and *how* until it is too late. We react to life as it unfolds, often not taking time to reflect until something major happens. This first Achiever Trait puts you in the proactive mode. Becoming a master of the question means incorporating the simple skill of questioning into your life to stop letting events just happen to you and to start making them happen *for* you.

If your questions aren't serving you, consider asking yourself different questions. For example, instead of asking "*Why* does this keep happening to me?," you might ask "*What* can I learn from this so it doesn't happen again?" Choose a new starting point. The more you ask yourself questions, the better you get at asking yourself the *right question* at the *right time.*

3. Being Honest with Your Answers

Asking the right question is only the first step. Listening honestly to the answer completes the picture. That sounds simple, but so many of us run from the truth. We don't want to face what is really going on because it might mean we have to change. But if we don't listen to ourselves honestly, we get stuck and start to spin our wheels.

The important thing to remember is that there are no wrong or right answers. Simply take the time to listen carefully for *your* truth. What is going on in your head? How do you feel? What do you really want? And where do you find yourself now? The answers might come quickly. In other cases, it might require some time. Enjoy taking that time in order to reflect and to listen to yourself.

DEBBIE: I have a great friend who has a hard time settling into employment. She joins a new company, but within six months to a year, the shine wears off and the same problems that occurred in her last place of employment reappear. She goes into a company and at first everything is great. Then, all of a sudden, she feels that people are turning against her. At first, I could completely sympathize with her. But then the next job came along and the same thing happened to her again. And when it happened a third time a year later, she needed to really ask herself some questions and be honest about the answers. Instead of it always being about the employer, she needed to ask the question, "What part am I playing in this?," and then honestly look at how to break this pattern.

ACHIEVERS

▲ TRAIT 1 REVIEW: Ask Yourself Questions

BEING A CHAMPION MEANS:
1. Understanding the Power of the Question
2. Knowing What to Ask Yourself When
3. Being Honest with Your Answers

KEY CONCEPT
By becoming a master of the question, you stay connected to yourself and to what you want to achieve.

REALITY CHECK!
We know that it can be kind of scary to ask yourself questions because you might not want to know what is going on. Sometimes it is easier just to go on autopilot because you might have to face an unpleasant truth, point the finger at yourself, or change something about what you are doing. But in order to achieve any win, it all starts by checking in regularly and asking yourself questions.

Bring This Trait to Life
Take some time to reflect. It can be a few minutes over coffee, or it can be a more in-depth period of time, like a personal retreat. The point is to give to yourself some space and time to reconnect to what is important for you. Here are a few questions to think about in relation to your personal and/or professional life:

▲ Am I happy with my current circumstances?
▲ What is working and what isn't working?
▲ How would I define a win in my life?

After listening honestly to what comes to you, consider what you might change or keep doing to reach whatever you have identified your next win to be.

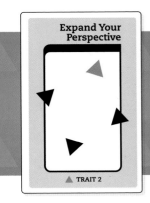

Expand Your Perspective

▲ TRAIT 2

TRAIT 2:
Expand Your Pespective

KEY CONCEPT

By looking at circumstances differently, you access new realms of possibility for yourself.

MARK: *In the weeks following the disaster at the Pan Pacifics where Jeff had broken the world record, I was invited to a wedding. Michelle Cameron, an Olympic synchronized swimming champion, was getting married to Al Coulter, an Olympic volleyball player. With ten months to go before the Olympics and absolutely no idea how I was ever going to reach my dream, I wasn't exactly in a celebrating mood. The idea of having hundreds of people from the world of sport ask me "How are things going?" was more than I could bear. I was dreading it. Before I even arrived, I had made up my mind that I wasn't going to have a good time.*

DEBBIE: Michelle had been one of my athletes, and it was at the wedding reception that I ran into Mark again. We hadn't really seen each other since our time together in Perth, and when I saw him, I could tell immediately that something wasn't right. Mark is usually very enthusiastic, but just from the way he said hello, I knew he wasn't himself. I

17

asked him if everything was okay, and he very honestly said no. He told me briefly about his setback, but he realized that it wasn't really the time or the place to get into it. So we set a date for lunch the following week.

MARK: *Seeing Debbie helped me get out of my funk for a few moments that night. There was something about being at Michelle's wedding, an Olympic champion, that helped me to see that it was actually humanly possible to be from Calgary, where I was living, and be a champion. But in terms of my own potential, I was still very limited in what I was thinking.*

One area that was enormously weak was my underwater technique that was essential to the start and turn—about 30 percent of my event. Because Debbie was an expert in this area, I thought that maybe when we had lunch, she could give me some tips about how to train better. I really had no idea what was about to happen.

DEBBIE: The first thing that struck me about Mark when we met for that unforgettable lunch was the fact that this guy wanted to win the Olympics more than any athlete I had seen. Listening to him talk, I could see that there were many things that he wasn't doing in his training. I started to see the possibility of what could happen if I helped him do some of those things. I knew it wouldn't be easy, but I remember thinking to myself, "This guy wants it so badly. He's got the ability. And he seems willing to do whatever it will take." As a coach, that combination was irresistible. I got really excited thinking that he could actually do this. And I shared that thought with Mark. He welled up with emotion.

I don't think either of us had expected the energy that would be created when we came together. Because when Mark saw that I genuinely thought he could do it, he completely opened to the possibility that he could make it happen for himself. As our lunch went into the three-hour mark, we could both see the possibility as clear as day. And once we saw it, there was no going back.

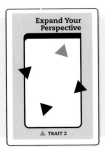

BEING A CHAMPION MEANS:
1. Noticing What You Notice
2. Knowing that a Narrow Perspective Is Limiting
3. Putting Things Back into Perspective

ACHIEVERS

1. Noticing What You Notice

It is human nature to have selective awareness. We set ourselves up to notice what we want to notice. Think about it. When you buy a new red car, what happens? You notice more red cars. What happens when you are pregnant? You suddenly notice other pregnant women. When you are trying to stop smoking, what do you see? People smoking everywhere! It is natural to focus our attention on what we are most conscious of. Without even realizing it, we go through the day seeing, hearing, feeling only what we have set ourselves up to see, hear, or feel. If we wake up in a bad mood, all day long we tend to give attention to events and people that reinforce how bad things are. And it is usually to the exclusion of everything else. Expanding perspective helps you to notice what you notice, and keeps you open to the things you might never have noticed before.

2. Knowing that a Narrow Perspective Is Limiting

Expanding perspective is the second Achiever Trait because it ensures that you don't box yourself in, both in terms of what is possible, and how you might get there. Realize that there is always more than one way to do anything. With expanded perspective, there is less chance of getting stuck, feeling frustrated or hopeless, or going down the wrong path because you could only see one solution. The decision might be to do the same thing over again, but that comes not from a place of limitation, but

ACHIEVERS

of choice. Increased perspective helps break the pattern of history repeating itself or making the same mistakes over and over again. It expands our ability to see different ideas, experiences, and choices, opening whole new realms of possibility for ourselves.

DEBBIE: Mary was incredibly smart, but she came to the world of coaching from the perspective of a chartered accountant. In her mind, unless something was perfect, it was wrong. From her point of view, everything was an absolute: 2 + 2 = 4. That was it. There was no room for deviation from this. But what that meant for the athletes she worked with was that something that was working 98 percent of the time was seen as failure, because it had to be either exactly right or it was wrong. Her swimmers were getting completely discouraged. I challenged Mary to only make positive comments about what she liked for two weeks. "But how are we going to get better if we aren't fixing what is wrong?" she argued. "Just try it," I responded. Two days later she called me. "It is like a miracle," she started. "Not only am I realizing that we are good at so many things, we are actually fixing what isn't working as I focus on what is." Her limited perspective was impacting those around her in the worst way imaginable. Shifting her perspective changed that.

3. Putting Things Back into Perspective

Many of us are living busy, busy lives, and in that busyness, sometimes we can lose perspective of all that we already do have. At times, we might feel pressure from every side, and even catch ourselves focusing only on what we don't have, or on what we haven't done, or on how good it might seem to be somewhere else. And then something happens. A friend takes ill. A sister gets pregnant. Something as simple as the beauty of the full moon or sunrise catches our attention. And without expecting it, our perspective is expanded. We get a little wake-up call that allows us to see things in a new way, and puts all that we do have back into perspective.

MARK: *One of my heroes had always been Victor Davis, largely because I saw with my own eyes this remarkable Canadian swimmer break world records and become an Olympic champion. He was a fierce competitor: brash, charismatic, pure raw talent. In my eyes, Victor was invincible. He was larger than life, and he had his entire future in front of him with unlimited possibility.*

I was running around the city doing errands one autumn day when I received the phone call. Victor had been out at a nightclub where he had had an ugly encounter with a small group of guys. As he left the club, they maliciously ran him down with their car. He never recovered. Just like that, at 25, he was dead. It was shocking. But it changed how I looked at things. It had always seemed like I had a long life ahead of me, that as a young person I was invincible just like Victor had been. Suddenly, every day took on a new meaning. I had a new perspective of just how precious life is.

ACHIEVERS

ACHIEVERS

▲ TRAIT 2 REVIEW: Expand Your Perspective

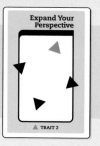

Expand Your
Perspective

▲ TRAIT 2

BEING A CHAMPION MEANS:
1. Noticing What You Notice
2. Knowing that a Narrow Perspective Is Limiting
3. Putting Things Back into Perspective

KEY CONCEPT
By looking at circumstances differently, you access new realms of possibility for yourself.

REALITY CHECK!
Sometimes the biggest factor holding us back is the way we see things. We limit our perspective about what is and isn't possible. Expanding your perspective means staying open to hear new ideas and see things you have never seen before. It also helps you put things that might have always been there back into perspective. It helps you seek out not only new possibilities in terms of what you can achieve; it connects you to different ways to make it happen.

Bring This Trait to Life
Shake things up a bit. Before reading any further, take 30 seconds, look around the room, and notice everything that is blue. Put this book down and count in your head how many things you see until the time is up. Ready, go.

Okay, so how many things did you see that were blue? How high did you count? Now, here is the catch. Without looking around the room again, how many things did you notice that were red?

The point here is that you only notice what you set yourself up to notice. We start our days looking for the blue to the exclusion of everything that is red. Start to notice what you notice as you go through your day. How is it potentially limiting you? Expanding your perspective will help you get to your win.

Make a Plan

TRAIT 3
▲ TRAIT 3

TRAIT 3:
Make a Plan

KEY CONCEPT
By laying the foundation for focused action, you create a clear path to take you to your desired win.

DEBBIE: Following our initial meeting over lunch, both Mark and I looked to the future with great excitement. But I knew that if this partnership was really going to work, we needed a solid plan to clearly map out exactly what we would need to do to make this dream happen. Planning is not the most exciting activity. In fact, with all of the details that we needed to consider, it was quite tedious. But this was a fundamental step in harnessing all of those good feelings that we shared into something more concrete.

MARK: *Year after year as an athlete, I had enjoyed slightly better results, so, to be honest, I had never even thought about creating a plan for myself. As long as I was improving, why should I bother planning? I just kind of chugged along, letting one year follow the next, content to just let life happen. Besides, planning was my coach's job, and I simply followed the general plan he made for the team that I was training with.*

When I found myself in the place where I had to make seven years' improvement in less than ten months, all of that changed. I couldn't rely on just letting life unfold as it had in the past. I needed my own specific plan to get myself to that higher level. Where that started was in clearly identifying what my goal was, and then charting a detailed path to get there.

It felt very strange to actually write down my objective for the first time. I wanted to become an Olympic champion, but that seemed such a stretch from anything that I had done in the past that it kind of freaked me out to see it in ink on paper. But, at the same time, it made me commit to it completely. The planning process was like a roller coaster. It was exciting to imagine the end result, depressing and scary to see where I was with only months to go, but hopeful as we started to identify all of the different things we were going to do to make it happen.

DEBBIE: Mark told me, "I want to do everything possible to be my best this year." That gave us a starting point to honestly assess all that needed to be done. I knew that as long as he had done everything possible, he could live with whatever the result proved to be. That was our guide.

The basic core element of swimming training was already taken care of. We looked at all of the different ways we could support that to make him better. There was technical work, strength, endurance, breath holding, and reaction time training. We broke down each of these ways into an intricate month-by-month, week-by-week, step-by-step process.

MARK: *Where in the past there had seemed to be an infinite amount of time to make this happen, I knew that if I didn't win these upcoming Olympics, then it wasn't ever going to happen. It forced me to plan. As much as I hated it at first, I came to realize how crucial the plan was. And once I understood how to create a thorough plan, it became something that I have done for myself every single year since.*

ACHIEVERS

BEING A CHAMPION MEANS:
1. Identifying Your Win
2. Seeing Where You Are Currently
3. Identifying What Needs to Be Done

1. Identifying Your Win

While anything is possible, getting there doesn't just happen on its own. For many of us, the process of planning is one that gets overlooked. We think we have it in our head and that should be good enough. But it isn't. Taking the time to thoughtfully outline a detailed roadmap ensures that we also take into account all of the different elements necessary to take us where we want to go.

We know this isn't the sexiest of our traits, but making a plan is the third Achiever Trait for a reason. It will be built upon later, and will ensure that the time you invest in planning will save countless hours in unfocused execution, creating an enormous return on investment. Remember, this is about the fundamentals. We know you've heard this before, but instead of rolling your eyes, make the plan! So where do we start?

The first step is to determine specifically what you want to achieve. The magnitude of your desired win will determine the scope of the process involved in getting there. Sometimes we might have a long-term objective, something that will require years to attain. Other times, it could be something within a relatively short time frame, like the next couple of weeks or months. In either case, the process doesn't change, only the scope does.

Every great plan begins with the end in mind, or at least with an idea of what the end will be. It is critical to ask yourself questions in order to make a great plan. Take the time to think about it carefully:

▲ What do you want?

▲ Where would you like to see yourself?

▲ How would you like to feel?

▲ What makes sense to you when you think about the future?

Write down your win once you have clearly identified it.

2. Seeing Where You Are Currently

Before you can get where you want to go, you need to see where you are in relation to your win. This sounds simple, but the tough part of breaking through is that you have to be brutally honest about where you are. This is not always easy. It requires us to face the sometimes harsh reality of where we find ourselves. Not unlike the process in the first Achiever Trait, Ask Yourself Questions, it is important to be completely honest here. Ensure that your planning genuinely reflects where you are right now—at this moment in time. Only then can you map out properly what needs to be done to get where you want to go.

DEBBIE: Every year, I faced the same situation with an athlete who couldn't understand why she didn't make the national team. Her downfall was her inability to be honest about her own talent and skill level. She always thought she was better than she actually was. In her mind, her poor results were always the judges' fault, or the coaches' fault. She could never look at the real work she needed to do because she thought she was already good enough. This unrealistic view of where she was, and, subsequently, the actions she would need to take, kept her back from ever achieving her win.

3. Identifying What Needs to Be Done

Since you know where you want to go, and you have been brutally honest about where you are, now you need to give your attention to all of the various actions that will go into completing the bigger picture. Remember, there is not just one thing or one way to get somewhere.

Identify some of the steps you immediately know will need to be done to move you forward. These are targets—small wins—that add up over time. In the short term, reaching for the next target gives you focus, keeping you from feeling overwhelmed. Targets are simply a series of small wins you need to make as you work toward achieving the overall objective. What are some of the various things you have to do to get from here to there? The planning process becomes an ongoing prioritized action plan. A plan provides clarity and, at the same time, allows room to be fluid, letting your actions shift and evolve as necessary along the way.

What you are left with following this simple process is something on paper that will act as your guide as you go forward. Many people keep their goals and plans in their heads. That can work, but why take the risk? The advantage to writing down what you want is that it also leads to writing down what you must do to get there. When you put it on paper, it clearly shows you the interconnectedness of the various aspects of what you will have to do.

DEBBIE: In order for Carolyn Waldo to become an Olympic champion, we decided that she needed to start her routine with the longest underwater sequence that had ever been done in the history of synchronized swimming. Where most athletes would stay under for 30 seconds, we were going for one minute. On top of that, we wanted to keep a high degree of difficulty right through to the end of her performance. We were clear about what we wanted to achieve, and we built a plan around that. We looked at all of the different types of training that would be needed so she could hold her breath longer than anyone else had in the world, and maintain her strength and power for the rest of her routine. Working backwards, we designed a two-year detailed program so that Carolyn would make it look easy once we got to the Olympics.

For a year and nine months, we worked diligently behind the scenes, following the targets that we had set for ourselves. With three months to go before the actual Games, we had a pre-Olympic competition where we unveiled the routine for the first time. The defending Olympic

ACHIEVERS

champion, Tracy Ruiz from the United States, was our main rival. At this competition, she saw how long Carolyn's underwater sequence was, and because of this, she went home and changed her routine, arriving at the Olympics with an even longer first underwater segment than Carolyn.

I felt sick the first time I saw Tracy practice the opening of her routine at the Olympics. That was until she came up for air and passed out in the water. She literally couldn't finish. I thought to myself, "Wow. Good thing we spent two years making ours work!" We had been clear about what we wanted, and had worked for years to make it happen. And it had paid off. Carolyn went on to win the Olympic gold medal. Tracy made it through the routine, but had to settle for second.

Planning is part vision—seeing what you want—but it leads to action, which is why it is so important to put time lines on your planning. The magic of taking the time to plan is that it assists you in doing the right thing at the right time to get you where you want to go. Tracy fell into a trap that is not uncommon. Most people don't allow themselves enough time to get where they want to go. Or they don't make the right plan in the first place. Planning made the difference between winning or not.

▲ TRAIT 3 REVIEW: Make a Plan

BEING A CHAMPION MEANS:
1. Identifying Your Win
2. Seeing Where You Are Currently
3. Identifying What Needs to Be Done

ACHIEVERS

KEY CONCEPT
By laying the foundation for focused action, you create a clear path to take you to your desired win.

REALITY CHECK!
Sometimes it is overwhelming to look at all that needs to be done, to sit down and take the time needed to make a plan. We can't go anywhere because we are paralyzed. Or we don't want to even stop to think, we just want to go. But before you get to the action—whatever is your win—the first step is making a plan. It will help you become clear on exactly what needs to be done, and help you figure out a time line for when you need to do it. The plan will make your actions focused and meaningful.

Bring this Trait to Life
Think about a short-term goal that you would like to accomplish this week. It could be as easy as organizing your schedule (time is one of all of our greatest challenges), to writing an important report. Practice making a simple plan to see how this process actually works. Write down the short-term objective—what do you want to achieve over the next seven days? What could be your win? Next, write down what you need to do to achieve it. Put a time line for this week to take those necessary steps. What do you have to do today, tomorrow, the next day, and so on, until you have your plan for the week? This will help you to start prioritizing the small action steps that need to be done. Now act like a champion and get to it!

TRAIT 4:
Act Effectively

KEY CONCEPT

By aligning your day-to-day actions with your objectives,
you ensure that what you are doing will keep you on track.

MARK: *Debbie and I had met a few times over the weeks after we originally decided to work together in order to carefully plan out what we needed to do. It was on a Thursday morning, two weeks later, when we actually made it to the pool for the first time. Finally, we were going to get down to work. We had mapped out what we had to do, but the minute we went to implement our strategy, we ran into our first problem.*

DEBBIE: When Mark got in and showed me his underwater kicking technique and ability to hold his breath, I saw immediately that we had an even bigger challenge than we had realized. He was much weaker than I had thought he would be. Because Mark was a world-class swimmer, I had assumed that he had, at the very least, a basic foundation of underwater technical skill. He didn't. If this was going to work, we had to completely step away from the plan that we had just made and figure out a new starting place. In this case, it meant taking several steps

31

backwards to get Mark where he could be effective. It was a good wake-up call early in the process. This experience showed us that even though the plan was still hugely important, it was simply a guide that was only as good as our ability to adjust to reality. It was useful to have a detailed plan, but we had to pay close attention to what was working and what wasn't.

MARK: *For me, this was completely heartbreaking. I was already overwhelmed by how much we had to do. Then, to have a setback before I had even really started was brutal. But I learned something invaluable from the experience. In the past, I was often asked to do things but was never given a clear explanation about why. I felt like sometimes we were doing things just for the sake of doing them, and when I asked "Why are we doing this?," the response would be "Because." In this case, yes, we had to change things, but Debbie was great at explaining why. I understood that what we were doing was going to help us be more effective in the long run, even though it seemed at first like we were going backwards.*

DEBBIE: I am not going to downplay how much there was to do, because there was a lot. But I knew that just as we hadn't started at the right place, there would be other surprises along the way that we could not foresee. The important thing was to make the best decisions based on the feedback we were getting from Mark's results in training and competition. Until we actually started, we didn't have anything to respond to. If we had tried to barrel through and stay with the original plan, then Mark would not have made it.

We had to go back to a more rudimentary level that gave Mark the foundation to build the technique properly. This raised not only his skill set, but also his confidence. What was amazing was to see how quickly Mark started to improve once he got some successes behind him. That was something we hadn't planned. We caught up to our original schedule much faster than we thought we would.

BEING A CHAMPION MEANS:
1. Getting Started
2. Evaluating Your Actions
3. Making Effective Decisions

1. Getting Started

This is about putting your plan into action—following it when it works, finding the best way forward when it doesn't. The plan becomes the guide from which to evaluate your progress. But the important thing is to start. Until you have done something, you have no way to know how it is working because you have nothing to react to. Start!

Ultimately, acting effectively is doing what works. This sounds so simple. It's like a no-brainer. But this is often the place where glitches happen. It is a potential danger zone because we get so stuck in delivering the plan that we forget to pay attention to whether things are working or not. In that busyness, we neglect evaluating or observing whether our actions are really on track.

2. Evaluating Your Actions

A fundamental part of acting effectively is holding yourself accountable. Is what you are doing leading you to where you want to go or not? Again, it is being able to build on the first Achiever Trait—Ask Yourself Questions—to honestly assess if what you are doing is working or if you have to take a different approach. Take some time, preferably on a regular basis, to check in with yourself. Done frequently, this doesn't have to be arduous and painful, but instead will make sure you are on track.

DEBBIE: One of my main competitors once shared with me some of her ideas, specifically how she was going to integrate complex scientific concepts that I had never even heard of into her training regimen. By the time she was finished explaining what she was going to do, I thought to myself, "Oh man, she is incredible. We are going to be toast when we compete against her!" But when I saw her team swim three months later, I had never before seen such a disconnection between a plan and its execution. They lacked all of the major elements they needed to achieve. If there had been a gold medal for planning, she would have won. But in terms of delivering the goods, she completely missed the mark. Maybe she worked long days, maybe she worked hard, but her team certainly didn't do what they needed to do in order to be successful. It is one thing to have a plan, but if you aren't able to implement it effectively, you are missing the point. It is not just about execution, it is also about making sure you have planned properly. If you haven't, you might need to change the plan.

3. Making Effective Decisions

Ultimately, this is not about choosing what is right or wrong, but about finding the next step that works best. Based on your evaluation, don't be a prisoner of the plan. While the road map is hugely important, it is just there as a guide. Sometimes we get caught up in the "doing" of a plan and lose our intuition about whether it is working or not. Watch what your results tell you. Base your decision making on genuine feedback and not on wishful thinking. If something is working, consider why and how long it will work. If it isn't working, consider why and find another way.

MARK: *When I was a young swimmer just coming onto the national team, we went to train in the mountains of France for three weeks thinking we were doing leading-edge training to become champions. Altitude training was highly regarded, but because of its intense nature, was also somewhat controversial. Swimming in thin air had its benefits, like increasing the red blood cell count, which helped endurance, but we had to be carefully monitored to avoid severe overtraining. With a carefully mapped-out plan, off we went.*

The problem was that we based our plan on those of the East German and Chinese teams, before it had been confirmed officially that they had used drugs to help them recover in training. As each day went by, following their incredible regimen without the artificial aids, we began to slowly drop off from sheer exhaustion, one by one. At first, it was decided to stick to the plan, but as the seriousness of our poor planning became apparent, we were too slow to change and the damage had been done. For many of us, it took two years to fully recover from the overtraining that we had done. We had completely burned ourselves out. Our outcome was exactly the opposite of what had been intended.

ACHIEVERS

▲ TRAIT 4 REVIEW: Act Effectively

BEING A CHAMPION MEANS:
1. Getting Started
2. Evaluating Your Actions
3. Making Effective Decisions

KEY CONCEPT
By aligning your day-to-day actions with your objective, you ensure that what you are doing will keep you on track.

REALITY CHECK!
There is only so much time, resources, and energy in a day, so we have to maximize those by making effective decisions. Planning and action merge through effective decision making. Ask yourself, "Is what I am doing working, or not?" It is pretty simple. The plan gives us a context for our actions. Where some of us fall short is when we forget to check in with the plan and ourselves to honestly see where we are.

Bring this Trait to Life
Ask yourself at the end of the day, "Did today really matter?" Be honest with yourself. Did the actions you took today move you closer to your win? Did you learn something that moved you forward? Were your actions as efficient and effective as they could be? If they weren't, what can you do differently tomorrow to get you back on the winning track?

TRAIT 5:
Go the Distance

KEY CONCEPT

On the way to achieving your desired win, you must be ready to persist through tough times and periods of hard work.

MARK: *From the very beginning of our work together, Debbie and I essentially based our process on three fundamental steps. Step one was to focus intensely on training certain skills in isolation. Step two was to integrate those new skills back into my regular swimming regime. The final step was to bring those skills to competition, where there was a much higher degree of pressure. Making it through each phase proved to be harder than I imagined. The first time I used my improved underwater kicking technique in a race, I went too far and was disqualified. We were only allowed to stay under for 15 meters, and my kick was so strong that I went 18. It was a major disappointment.*

DEBBIE: It was really tough because we were trying so hard to prove to all of the doubters that what we were doing was working. Sometimes when you start something new, there is a little thought that says, "Okay, this is going to be magic. We'll show all those people who don't believe." And then it hurts like hell when not only do you not show

37

them, you actually prove them temporarily right. That was when we really had to find the positive advances and believe in what we were doing. Yes, Mark went too far off the start in the competition. But it was because his underwater technique was so much better, which meant we were on the right track. It took some time to make the many adjustments we needed to make, but Mark never gave up, even though most people around him remained skeptical.

MARK: *Not giving up took on a whole new meaning later that year. For three weeks over Christmas, my team traveled to Australia for a training camp. Because the Olympics were in an outdoor pool in Barcelona and our pool at home was indoors, we needed to invest some time training under the sun to get used to it. It was there that we met a coach who specialized in endurance training. I had known periods of long, hard work before, but I had never before experienced anything like this. We did something called a heart rate set. Essentially, we were asked to get our heart rates to 180 beats per minute (bpm), and then keep it there for an hour. In a typically challenging set, my heart rate might peak at 180 to 200 bpm, but for much, much shorter periods of time. Keeping it at 180 bpm for an hour was unheard of, even for elite athletes. It was the most intense session I had ever been asked to do in my life.*

In order to get the most out of the set, not only did I do the long, painful swimming, I also integrated the underwater technique that I had been doing with Debbie into the workout. It was the combination of the hour-long intense set, working on the underwater dolphin kick off the start and turn on every single length, and learning to cope with the paralyzing buildup of lactic acid in my system that compounded the results of this set for me.

DEBBIE: Part of the focus that year was to get through the monotonous drudgery of the day-to-day training. This is where you get to show who you are and what you are made of, and it is where, unfortunately, so many people give up. Were there times when it wasn't pretty? Absolutely there were, especially during some of those long, dark days of January, February, and March. But getting through those times was a fundamental part of the process.

MARK: *Something that helped me make it through was to constantly celebrate the little improvements along the way. When I first swam underwater for 15 meters straight, we cheered. Over time, I saw that we were making major gains. At the Winter Nationals, I broke the Canadian record. But I still knew there was no guarantee that I was going to eventually win my race at the Olympics. We didn't wait to enjoy that moment in the future; we made sure to celebrate the process along the way. It was these moments that made the hard work tolerable.*

BEING A CHAMPION MEANS:
1. Never Giving Up
2. Paying Attention to the Details
3. Enjoying the Journey

1. Never Giving Up

Going the distance means you endure the drudgery, you overcome the challenges, you put in the time. Where planning provides the road map, it is the long-term commitment of acting effectively over time that ultimately turns possibility into results.

The daily grind, the slog, the routine is the part that sometimes isn't so much fun. Getting up at 5 a.m. and enduring a -40 degree trip to the pool, only to jump into freezing water for a two-hour swim before school, was sometimes brutal. Unfortunately, there was no way around it. This is where many of us look for the shortcuts, hoping for an easier way. Then, one of two things usually happens. Either we give up, thinking we'll try something else that is easier, or worse, we throw out the plan and drastically reduce our expectations, settling for something less. Unfortunately, there is no avoiding the periods of long, hard work.

2. Paying Attention to the Details

Going the distance isn't just about showing up, going on autopilot, and putting in long, sloppy hours. It is about being focused, thinking of the thousands of little things that need to be well done along the way that, in the end, accumulate to get you where you want to go. Incorporating the small things and paying attention to those details while doing the long, hard work is where results start to get compounded.

Working effectively over time creates a trajectory that takes you from where you are to where you want to be. The details add up along the way, strengthening our foundation one small step at a time. Fundamentally, these two aspects ensure that you are not only putting in the time, but you are also digging deeper and doing everything possible to make your win come to life.

3. Enjoying the Journey

Getting to the final goal, your win, is the ultimate objective. At the end of the day, achievements will come and go, but the process will stay with you forever. It can be easy to let the routine grind us down. But the small progress, the baby steps along the way—that is where the real learning lies. Surprisingly, these are the moments that often stand out years later when we look back. When we get together with people and reflect, don't we often reminisce about the day-to-day challenges we overcame together? The win was great, but often the trip was even better.

MARK: *In the late 1980s, I was part of a small group of athletes who were let inside the Soviet Union to train with the Russians. For three weeks, we resided on the coast of the Black Sea, across from Turkey, at a resort where politicians and athletes were given exclusive access.*

I learned some important things there. As much drudgery as there was—the same meals three times a day, shared bathrooms, a hard physical routine—there were always periods of rest, recovery, and fun built in. Who knew it would be the Russians who would teach me to find enjoyment? In the middle of the afternoon swimming session, hot tea, honey, and biscuits would arrive. We would all finish the set we were doing and take a break together. I came to love these times. It was much needed food energy, but also a moment to joke around and laugh with each other with body language, hand signals, and broken English and Russian. It was where the friendships were built. I left Russia knowing that I had put all of this effort into something, and that regardless of what happened in the future, it had been a meaningful experience that I could look back on and celebrate. Times like those gave me the strength to go the distance.

ACHIEVERS

ACHIEVERS

▲ TRAIT 5 REVIEW: Go the Distance

BEING A CHAMPION MEANS:
1. Never Giving Up
2. Paying Attention to the Details
3. Enjoying the Journey

KEY CONCEPT
On the way to achieving your desired win, you must be ready to persist through tough times and long periods of hard work.

REALITY CHECK!
It is easy at first to be excited about tackling a new challenge. But as time wears on and fatigue, frustration, disappointment, reality, and stress all start to appear—and they do appear en route to every achievement at some point—it becomes very important not to give up. Besides, more often than not, it is how we did it that we take forward. The results come and go, but the process of going for our wins, big and small, stays with us forever. It is the capacity to persevere, to overcome the odds and obstacles, that makes getting there so rewarding.

Bring this Trait to Life
We invite you to take the 21-day challenge. The only way to go the distance is with time, so this fun exercise asks you to commit. Choose something that you know you will need to do in order to reach one of your objectives, but you have been putting it off for whatever reason. Commit to doing something about that for the next 21 days in a row. Take a calendar and mark each day that you take action. It could be 5 minutes a day; it could be a couple of hours. The choice is yours. The point here is to be a champion and go the distance. Watch the calendar numbers climb to 21, and pay attention to how your efforts accumulate.

TRAIT 6:
Be Innovative

KEY CONCEPT

By challenging yourself to tap into new solutions, you find unique ways to move forward.

DEBBIE: It had taken the crisis of the Pan Pacific Games to bring Mark and me to work together. We had been on the same pool deck hundreds of times, Mark coming to watch my athletes train, and me to see him compete, but we had never before made the connection that we could benefit from working together. Sometimes, innovation is like that—it is just connecting ideas, experiences, or knowledge in a way that has never been done before. Simply by working together that year, Mark and I were being innovative.

MARK: *There wasn't any one single moment of acting with innovation that stands out from that time. It was more like a creative mindset that took over that year, eventually becoming a way of being that enabled us to generate many ideas and take innovative actions. That outlook kept building on itself throughout the year to find solutions to problems as they arose.*

DEBBIE: When we realized that we needed to strengthen Mark's legs to support the technical work we were doing, there was no way to simulate that specific training in the weight room. So what did we do? We brought the weights right into the water. I tied 25 pounds onto a piece of tubing, and then tied that around Mark's waist. He sank to the bottom of the pool. The challenge was to push off from there and kick vertically to the surface, the goal being to get his chest out of the water. The first time we tried it, I thought I was going to have to get the lifeguard to save him. He could barely break the surface of the water with his mouth, let alone his chest. But, eventually, he got it. It was simply a matter of finding better ways of doing things in order to achieve the objective.

MARK: *I was in Vancouver for a competition three months before Barcelona. A couple of people I was staying with decided to go and see if they could get tickets to the U2 concert that night. Normally, I wouldn't have gone, but one of my friends noted that the stadium held approximately 12,000 people. Something clicked. That was the expected capacity crowd for the final of the 100-meter backstroke at the Olympics.*

One of my challenges that year was to do something to prepare myself for the energy that tens of thousands of people would create. I had been to an Olympics before, and had been overwhelmed by the enormity of everything. I thought this would be a great way to get over that and feel more comfortable. That night, every time Bono introduced a song and the huge mass of people roared, I took in that energy, thinking not about the upcoming song, but pretending that I was standing on the starting blocks looking out at the crowd. I had never done anything like this before. New thinking led to more confidence.

Be Innovative

▲ TRAIT 6

BEING A CHAMPION MEANS:
1. Making Innovation Simple
2. Generating New Ideas
3. Having the Courage to Take Risks

1. Making Innovation Simple

Innovation is like a blank slate. With it, anything can happen. It invites us to go past what we know, breaks the boredom of routine, and gives us an edge in navigating around the roadblocks that appear. It encourages us to explore, imagine, and create in order to find solutions to the challenges that arise en route to wherever we want to go.

Many people don't see themselves as creative or innovative because they aren't in a creative industry. But if you have traveled with kids, you are innovative—or you'd go crazy! If you are in a long-term relationship and are still happy and having fun, then you must certainly know about innovation. The point here is that innovation doesn't have to be complicated. It can be simple, but it keeps things interesting and exciting, and it has the capacity to break through to new and better ways of doing things.

2. Generating New Ideas

This trait builds on the ideas found in the second Achiever Trait, Expand Your Perspective, but this time, instead of just seeing things from a different perspective, innovation asks you to make connections that you might have never made before and go the next step by taking action. The point is to create combinations that have never existed, translating them into unique solutions and outcomes.

MARK: *Going into the Olympics can be intimidating. In the final days before leaving North America for Europe, Debbie was asked to work with a group of female athletes, specifically to help them build their confidence. Her challenge was to help the women learn to deal with those potential overwhelming feelings that can come when you find yourself surrounded by the best athletes in the world. Instead of doing a boring workshop in a hotel room, she decided to use the environment around her in a unique way. Since they were training in Los Angeles, what could be better than Beverly Hills?*

It turned out to be the perfect training ground for creating the confidence needed when you are surrounded by the best of the best. Five of them crammed into a cheap little car that Debbie rented, and off they went to Rodeo Drive. The whole idea was to look confident even if they didn't necessarily feel it, because they might need that skill when arriving at the Games. None of them felt that comfortable buzzing to be let in to the ultra exclusive shops, or asking to see a piece of jewelry worth hundreds of thousands of dollars. It was absolutely intimidating! But that was exactly the situation Debbie was looking for. It gave the athletes the chance to do something out of their comfort zone. An innovative solution gave the girls a fun experience that helped them overcome the insecure feelings they might have in the Olympic environment. In fact, when they got to Barcelona, they couldn't stop smiling as the stress mounted, thinking of what they had done on Rodeo Drive.

3. Having the Courage to Take Risks

The point here is to take calculated risks, not stupid ones. Being innovative just for the sake of being innovative isn't effective. It could actually be destructive. This can be where some of us get carried away. We might constantly be throwing ourselves at new and different things, but if it isn't getting us closer to where we want to go, we might simply be spinning our wheels. Constructive innovation means finding effective solutions that work.

DEBBIE: I was three months out from the Olympics and I knew our synchronized swimming team had a problem. Our routine was great—technically excellent with a high degree of difficulty—but it was missing a punch at the end. We had set the routine to the music from Spartacus, which was serious and compelling, but it wasn't going to get the crowd on their feet. In order to win, it became clear that we would have to get the crowd on our side. So, to everyone's shock, we changed the music. We set the last third of the routine to Offenbach's popular theme, "The Can/Can." It raised the energy level at the end way up. It was virtually unheard of to do this—not only changing the music so late in the game, but also mixing these two completely different styles together. It just wasn't something you did. However, looking at what would happen if we didn't innovate, it was a calculated risk that made sense. We ended up winning the Olympic gold medal.

▲ TRAIT 6 REVIEW: Be Innovative

BEING A CHAMPION MEANS:
1. Making Innovation Simple
2. Generating New Ideas
3. Having the Courage to Take Risks

KEY CONCEPT

By challenging yourself to tap into new solutions, you find unique ways to move forward.

REALITY CHECK!

It can be easy to do things the same way we have always done them, finding ourselves getting stuck at the same place. But with innovation, that doesn't need to happen. Are you open to seeing things that you have never seen before, and then acting on them? Just using your experience, skills, and knowledge to find a creative solution to a problem that arises can be an innovation. Keep an open mind and see it work for you.

Bring this Trait to Life

Take a problem or challenge that you are currently facing, and for 10 minutes generate a list of solutions. Don't judge, just write. Be as imaginative and "out there" as you can. The point here is to generate as many ideas as possible. Make them crazy, seemingly impossible, whatever. Now let all the ideas float in your head for a day or two. Then, choose one solution and act on it.

Utilize Power
of Thought

▲ TRAIT 7

TRAIT 7:
Utilize Power of Thought

KEY CONCEPT
By mastering your thoughts, you have a much greater
chance of accessing your full potential.

DEBBIE: After a couple of months of working together, I began to notice that although Mark and I were doing some great training, we weren't getting the most out of our workouts. Something wasn't right. Having coached many champions before, I could hear from the way Mark was talking that he wasn't *thinking* like a champion. Many times he just seemed to lack the confidence he would need to be the best in the world. One afternoon after a workout, I asked him pointedly, "Mark, why *can't* you beat Jeff Rouse?" I was expecting him to respond positively, that there *was* no reason why he couldn't win. Instead we both gained a huge insight into what was running through his mind by his response.

MARK: *Before I could stop myself, I came out with ten different reasons why I didn't think that I could do it. To be honest, I didn't even realize that all of these negative thoughts had been there. They had been boiling under the surface, and finally they came into consciousness for* *me. Over time, these subconscious thoughts had reinforced this belief that I couldn't win the Olympics. This thinking was holding me back from being completely engaged, and it was having a negative impact on my physical preparation. Now that I was aware of it, we could do something to change that.*

Whenever we had spoken about winning, that little voice in my head would say, "But you've never won the Olympics or World Championships before. When the big one comes, you have always just missed out. What makes you think you can do it now?" Unveiling this self-talk immediately took away some of its power. Simply facing it gave me confidence. We identified the problem: I needed to change this limited thinking, and for the rest of the year, we made sure my thinking was working for me, not against me.

DEBBIE: Mark really opened up, sharing anything that came to his mind that he thought might be holding him back. With about five months to go before the Barcelona Olympics, he told me that he was really having a hard time imagining himself winning. Whenever he thought of the Olympics, he reverted to his experience of the past where he had missed the medal podium. We came up with a plan to change that.

Before my athletes became Olympic champions, we had gone to see the venues and get a feel for the city in which they would compete— Seoul in 1988. It was at a time when the pressure of the Olympics wasn't upon them, and we could have some fun and enjoy the city. It turned out to be a great idea. When we went back for the actual Games, there was a familiarity, and even a bit of recognition, from the Korean public. We thought the same thing would work really well for Mark if he went to Barcelona early.

MARK: *So that was what I did. I went to Barcelona and walked the long rambling boulevards, taking in the energy of the people out in the streets, and completely connected with the city. I went to the Olympic pool, which was still under construction, but imagined myself racing* *there in five months' time. It was an incredible experience because from that moment forward, I thought of the Olympics and I felt good. I could visualize myself winning instead of being stuck in the results of the past. When I actually got to the Olympics in July, I had a déjà vu, because I had already been there in person, and then again hundreds of times in my mind. It gave me a secret competitive edge.*

DEBBIE: Mark and I were doing all of this detailed, thorough work, but it was right before he left Canada for the final ten weeks of training that we really paid our full attention to the mental preparation. Mark was given a workbook filled with visualization, affirmation, and script writing exercises by a sport psychologist, which we almost ignored. It just goes to show how easy it is to overlook the mental part of the journey.

One evening when we returned home from dinner, we decided to take a few minutes and look at the workbook. For fun, we just started flipping through it. Mark did one exercise and before you knew it, we were completely engrossed. The sun was rising as we finished. It would turn out to be one of the most important final details.

MARK: *It started with some affirmations: "I am fast. I am strong. I am fit. I am gutsy." At first, I thought it was a bit of a joke, but as the powerful words kept coming, I started to get into it. So I kept going. I wrote out the people on the team who I would use for support, challenges I might face, and solutions or ideas to remember if they arose. The highlight was using words to create a script for my race. "I see myself FOCUSED in the warm-up. I feel GORGEOUS. I am SPECTACULAR. We are called for the race and I feel EXCITED and EMPOWERED. I walk to my lane and SMILE. I am READY. I swim PERFECTLY. I look at the scoreboard and feel MONUMENTAL. I have performed my BEST, EVER. I am PROUD. I have WON." For the next ten weeks, I read and re-read the things I had written in this workbook, over and over. I was one of the only swimmers who took it seriously. Ten weeks later, my thoughts came to life.*

BEING A CHAMPION MEANS:
1. Knowing What Is Running Through Your Head
2. Understanding Your Thoughts to Shape Beliefs
3. Using Your Thoughts to Drive Your Actions

1. Knowing What Is Running Through Your Head

En route to getting what we want, most of us focus on what we have to *do*, and pay very little attention to what we have to *think*. The fundamental part of this trait is to understand that our actions—what we do and how we do it—are direct products of what we think all day long. The funny thing is, most of us don't ever stop to *think about this*.

By some estimates, we have 60,000 thoughts a day, most at the subconscious level. Of these thoughts, 80 percent are about ourselves. And approximately two-thirds of these self-centered thoughts are negative in nature. That is 31,000 negative thoughts a day! To make matters worse, we tend to have the same thoughts day after day after day. This explains why it can be so hard to get ourselves out of a rut. Don't leave your thinking at the subconscious level. Start to become aware of what is running through your head.

2. Understanding Your Thoughts to Shape Beliefs

Over time, the repetition of our thoughts becomes deep-seated beliefs that tell us what we can and cannot do. If we leave our thinking submerged at the subconscious level, this is where we also unwittingly leave our belief for what is possible for ourselves. There is a deep interconnectedness between our thoughts and our beliefs.

How can we become more aware of that connection?

There are some key factors that help shape what our belief system ultimately becomes. Through understanding how those factors work, we are more able to use our thoughts to create an empowering belief.

▲ Self-Talk
Supposedly we talk to ourselves all of the time except for 11 seconds an hour. That's a lot of talking, and most of it is happening at the subconscious level. That mental chitchat is called self-talk and it has to go somewhere, and that is likely your belief system. Start to notice what you are saying to yourself. What messages are you reinforcing?

▲ Our Own Verbal and Non-Verbal Language
Our thoughts take the form of words and actions. Listen to the words you are using—what you are saying, what you are thinking, what you are writing—as well as paying attention to the messages your actions are giving. Are they limiting and negative in nature, or positive and empowering?

▲ Others Verbal and Non-Verbal Language
What other people say and do to us can have a profound impact on our own thinking and, ultimately, on our belief system. What they say might sneak in below our level of consciousness and start to play with our thinking, unbeknownst to us. Pay attention! Don't let the negative view of others shape what you believe is possible for yourself.

▲ Our Experiences and Our Own Unique Interpretation of Them
Every experience we have produces some kind of thought, again often at the subconscious level. Be aware! Don't let the past shape the future unless you want it to. Just because something happened once doesn't mean it has to happen again.

3. Using Your Thoughts to Drive Your Actions

There is a mind–body connection that is so obvious that many of us don't realize its implications. Every thought and belief is connected in some way to our physiology. What we think is literally what we get. Here is how it works:

ACHIEVERS

The Thought Cycle

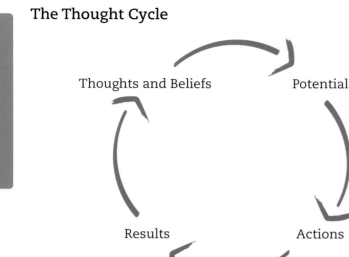

The Thought Cycle is simple: Our thoughts and beliefs unlock our potential, influencing directly just how much we can or cannot access. This in turn initiates what actions we take, which then produces a certain result. This result reinforces our thoughts and beliefs, bringing us right back to the beginning of the cycle.

Often, our results reinforce what we already know to be true, creating an ongoing sequence for ourselves. The goal is to make the Thought Cycle positive.

If you are not getting the results you are looking for, you need to do things differently. Sometimes this will mean changing actions—*what you are doing*. Sometimes it means changing your thoughts—*what you are thinking*. The goal is to create an empowering Thought Cycle that brings you success.

The exciting thing is that we don't have to be at the mercy of our subconscious thoughts. We can develop our mental capacity to get the kind of results we are looking for. There are numerous techniques that we can master. Here are three to start:

▲ Become More Aware

Acknowledging your thoughts (and, therefore, your beliefs) and whether they are limiting or empowering is often enough to change them. At the very least, becoming more aware of what is running through your head will show what thoughts or actions you might need to change to break a negative cycle.

▲ Take Control of Words

We can train our thoughts by consciously deciding what words we use. Just like repeating an action over time makes it second nature—covering your mouth when you yawn is an example—so, too, can we repeat our thoughts to become second nature and empowering.

Words are at the heart of affirmations and scripts. When we take the time to consciously write out what we would like to see, feel, or hear at any given time with strong, empowering language, and then read that back to ourselves, those ideas sink into our subconscious, changing how we act over time.

▲ Use Imagination

Visualization, long practiced in the world of sport, is a powerful tool to create the results we are seeking. Essentially, we imagine in as much detail as possible the positive outcome we want to happen. This might conjure up a picture in your mind, or a feeling in your body, or tap into your other senses in some way. Use visualization to see the invisible and imagine the impossible.

DEBBIE: I was sitting in the bleachers by myself, staring at the blue water of the empty Olympic-size pool. As I watched, the pool came alive. We were on the deck getting ready for the finals at the Olympics. I was talking to the swimmers just prior to them getting in and warming up. We looked relaxed and happy. We were confident.

The competition approached. The judges were in place, and the announcer said, "And now representing Canada...." There was a buzz. The entire stadium fell silent. The athletes took their positions and the music began. They dove into the water and did a 50-second underwater sequence of unimaginable difficulty. As they surfaced, the crowd roared. There was electricity in the air. I felt relieved watching as perfection unfolded in front of me.

As the swimmers finished, the audience was on its feet. The noise was deafening. In my heart, I knew that we were the best. The marks flashed. The crowd roared. I heard the music for the medal ceremony. "Ladies and gentlemen, the Olympic champions from Canada...." I watched proudly as the flag was raised and the anthem was played. We had won the Olympics!

I had played this scene in my mind thousands of times. Eight years later, it became reality.

▲ TRAIT 7 REVIEW: Utilize Power of Thought

BEING A CHAMPION MEANS:
1. Knowing What Is Running Through Your Head
2. Understanding Your Thoughts to Shape Beliefs
3. Using Your Thoughts to Drive Your Actions

KEY CONCEPT
By mastering your thoughts, you have a much greater chance of accessing your full potential.

REALITY CHECK!
Sometimes, we are not getting the results we are looking for because our thinking gets in the way. This is not as simple as think positive and everything will be okay, although there is a hint of truth there. This trait is about becoming the architect of your thinking. Increase your chances of success by paying attention to the thoughts that are running through your head.

Bring this Trait to Life
To illustrate the mind–body connection, try this fun exercise. Take a 10-inch piece of string and tie one end of it around the top loop of a paper clip. Holding the string between your thumb and index finger, and with your elbow resting firmly on a table, let the paper clip hang down naturally. Staring at the paper clip, and without letting your arm move, begin to imagine in your mind the paper clip swinging side to side. In your mind's eye, you see it starting to move from left to right, swinging bigger and bigger. What is happening to the paper clip? Simply by imagining it, the paper clip starts moving from side to side. Play this up a bit. Have some fun with it. Imagine the clip moving forward and backward, and then in a circle. You will be amazed at the power your thoughts have in determining your actions. What you think is what you get.

TRAIT 8:
Generate Enthusiasm

KEY CONCEPT

Since we rarely win anything alone, by sharing your passion and excitement, you invite others to be a part of the journey.

MARK: *As we wrap up the Achiever Traits, I have a confession to make. While you might imagine a top male athlete as being masculine, virile, and tough, at heart I also was (and remain) hyper—kind of a big goof. Everyone on my swimming team always knew they could count on me to lighten things up, insert some energy, and have a good laugh when we needed it. As I moved through my athletic career, I knew that this was an asset. In the months leading up to the Olympics, I learned how to capitalize on this by creating more energy through what I was doing.*

DEBBIE: When your ultimate objective is based around a specific day or moment in time, there can be an enormous amount of pressure that accompanies that. It is not uncommon to feel terrified as it approaches. But you can find ways to turn this around, especially by looking for ways to purposefully generate enthusiasm. For example, we knew that Mark's race was going to be on a Thursday. Around three months before the Olympics, we decided to make Thursdays the day of the week that he would really look forward to. We made it like a performance day, meaning that there was some pressure built into the training, and at the same time, we linked it to fun. We would go for a dinner, a coffee, a movie, whatever. At first, Mark was overtired and dreaded doing something fun. But, with time, when Mark woke up on a Thursday, he would automatically know that something challenging but good and fun was going to happen to him.

MARK: *I had never considered that you could consciously create fun at work, but that was exactly what we did in that Olympic year. And it spread well beyond the pool.*

Many amateur athletes have a real challenge supporting themselves financially, and I was no exception. Following my first Olympics, I started speaking to school kids to share some of my experiences. Because I was not a bad storyteller—hyper and goofy came in handy!— I was a hit with the kids. Word spread and eventually led to my speaking to business groups, which ultimately led to supporting my athletic career financially. What I hadn't anticipated was the kind of energy that would come back to me from all of these people with whom I had shared my excitement. In the months leading up to my second Games, I received letters of support from thousands of people who felt a part of my journey. It was an incredible feeling to know that I had all of these people rooting for me. My outlook and attitude had made an impression on them, and came back to me in a way that I could have never anticipated.

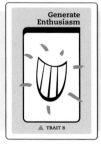

Generate Enthusiasm

▲ TRAIT 8

BEING A CHAMPION MEANS:
1. Understanding that Your Attitude Sets the Tone
2. Creating a Positive Ripple Effect
3. Paying Attention to What Comes Back

1. Understanding that Your Attitude Sets the Tone

Most of the Achiever Traits have focused on you—how you are thinking, acting, and being. It was all about YOU. The reality is that we rarely achieve anything in isolation. The environment we create with our attitude and outlook will be what draws other people to support us. Essentially, our attitude sets the tone. When we are excited about what we are doing, other people tend to get excited, too, and will do what they can to be a part of it. It is very important to understand the role our attitude plays in connecting to success.

Some people believe that you can't have fun and do great work. We think the exact opposite is true. If we are not having fun, then why bother? Fun creates energy. Energy begets energy, which means that more gets done. Momentum builds. And from that, success is more likely to follow. It is a situation in which everyone benefits because regardless of the final outcome, you had a great time along the way.

2. Creating a Positive Ripple Effect

The energy that we put into whatever pursuit we undertake affects the people and environment around us. Unfortunately, this idea works both ways.

If you are passionate, eager, absorbed, captivated, motivated, inspired, and care deeply about what you are doing, then chances are that those around you will feel the same way. They get caught up in those emotions with you. If you are detached, uninspired, disengaged, unhappy, pessimistic, and negative, then chances are that you will attract others with similar dispositions. Negative or positive—what kind of ripple are you creating from the way you are behaving?

3. Paying Attention to What Comes Back

When you are enthusiastic and passionate about something and put that energy out in the world, the most incredible thing happens. You start to attract people, circumstances, and opportunities that support what you are doing. Look at it this way:

Think of an Australian boomerang. What excites you about what you are doing? When you share that with others, you are essentially "throwing it out there." See what comes back to you.

Why is this important? There are going to be times when things get tough. In those dark moments, it is often the energy of those who we have shared our original passion with that comes back to us. That returned interest and support reminds us why we are doing what we are doing in the first place. Essentially, it is our enthusiasm that boomerangs back to us and refuels the dream, and can ultimately ensure that we keep going.

MARK: *Growing up in the world of swimming, with competitions weekend after weekend after weekend, could quickly get really boring. But if people from my club were competing, I would always give them a clap or a cheer of encouragement. It started really small, but it was amazing how many people joined in, too. Then, whenever I went to swim, many of those I had cheered on were there to support me. This energy followed me every step of my swimming career, right through to the national team. It was exciting watching your friends going for their best, and getting behind them with applause. And it was equally as exciting when competition time came for me and I heard people cheering for me above the roar of those supporting a competitor.*

▲ TRAIT 8 REVIEW: Generate Enthusiasm

Generate
Enthusiasm

▲ TRAIT 8

BEING A CHAMPION MEANS:
1. Understanding that Your Attitude Sets the Tone
2. Creating a Positive Ripple Effect
3. Paying Attention to What Comes Back

KEY CONCEPT
Since we rarely win anything alone, by sharing your passion and excitement, you invite others to be a part of the journey.

REALITY CHECK!
We know that winning can seem like a singular pursuit. But, our attitude and outlook can create excitement in many around us, supporting what we are doing in ways that we can't even imagine. Think about it. Who wouldn't rather have that collective universal energy of many, many people cheering you on and working for you instead of against you? It is the fun and the sharing of energy that connects you to higher levels of performance, and ultimately to your win.

Bring this Trait to Life
What are you really excited about? And whom do you share it with? All of us need a cheering squad, from a close friend to office mates. Take some time to think about it, clearly identifying what it is that gets your energy flowing in a positive way. Now, share it with whomever you choose to be in the cheering squad. Watch to see where that energy, excitement, and enthusiasm takes you.

THE FINAL ACHIEVEMENT
Becoming a Champion
The short story before each of the eight Achiever Traits showed how these fundamental ideas guided us in the ten months leading up to the Barcelona Olympics. All of the year's efforts had been focused toward July 30, the day of the 100-meter backstroke final. Here is what happened.

MARK: *When I woke up on that morning, I knew instinctively that something good was going to happen. I could hardly wait for it to come! In the first round, there had been sixty-five of us competing in the preliminaries. Fifty-seven swimmers were eliminated, and the top eight came back nine hours later to swim for the medals in the final. The first thing I did when I got back to the Olympic village was to call Debbie in Calgary. Unfortunately, she wasn't able to be in Barcelona.*

DEBBIE: It was 5 a.m. when the phone rang. Mark had qualified for the 100-meter backstroke final in second place, and we spoke for the last time before he would swim his race that night. I was as nervous and excited as he was. When we had first started this journey less than a year ago, it had been Mark's absolute commitment and enthusiasm that I couldn't resist. I knew what was at stake for Mark, and how much time and energy had gone into this. It was very nerve-racking.

Having been to the Olympics, I knew how stressful those last 24 hours are before the race. It can be really easy to forget the part that is fun. So I had made a little surprise for Mark. Weeks earlier, I sat down and wrote him a letter that was only to be opened the night before the race. In it, I showed him how much I believed in him, and did it in a way that I knew would make him laugh. And remind him that he could do this.

MARK: *I was carrying that letter with me all day. For most of the time before the final, I just rested back in my room in the Olympic village. Many thoughts went through my mind, but it would ultimately be a question that popped into my head and got me focused. "Someone has to win this race tonight. Why not me?" It jolted me upright in my bed. Usually, I would have thought about all of the things that I didn't do. This would be the time that I would defeat myself, noticing only what I hadn't done, letting my own insecurities take over. But this year had been so different. I had worked with Debbie. We had made a plan that outlined all of the different things I needed to do to get there. I had made it through the brutal training sessions, including the heart rate set in Australia, that I knew gave me the endurance I would need at the end of the race that night.*

I asked myself again, "Why not me?" I thought of coming to Barcelona early, of preparing for the crowds that night, of the mental skills workbook that had gotten me through some low points in the final weeks of preparation. I thought of the thousands of people who were cheering for me around the world.

One last time, I asked myself, "Why not me?" No answer came. So I repeated the words back to myself very slowly. "Why – not – me!"

I went back to the pool that night and swam the 100-meter backstroke final. When I looked to the scoreboard for the results, I don't remember seeing the time or the placing. The only thing I saw was that on the big Olympic screen, with all of the eight finalists' names, it was mine—Mark Tewksbury—that blinked first. Eventually, I saw the time— 53.98! We'd found the 1.2 seconds we'd been looking for. My dream had come true. I had the performance of my life in the moment it most mattered. I won the race in Olympic record time, and won my country's first gold medal of the Games.

One of the highlights of what followed included the victory march around the pool. I had been around a long time, but never connected to the win on the big day. As I came to the part of the stadium where the other swimmers were sitting, one by one the teams from different countries of the world, my peers, rose and cheered, "Bravo Mark!" I had to hold back the tears. Debbie and I had imagined an impossible win. We had done it!

ACHIEVERS

KEY CONCEPT SYNOPSIS
THE ACHIEVER TRAITS
Fundamentals for Being a Champion

 By becoming a master of the question, you stay connected to yourself and to what you want to achieve.

 On the way to achieving your desired win, you must be ready to persist through tough times and periods of hard work.

 By looking at circumstances differently, you access new realms of possibility for yourself.

 By challenging yourself to tap into new solutions, you find unique ways to move forward.

 By laying the foundation for focused action, you create a clear path to take you to your desired win.

 By mastering your thoughts, you have a much greater chance of accessing your full potential.

 By aligning your day-to-day actions with your objectives, you ensure that what you are doing will keep you on track.

 Since we rarely win anything alone, by sharing your passion and excitement, you invite others to be a part of the journey.

ACHIEVER TRAITS—SELF ASSESSMENT

Before moving on in this book, take the time to complete this quick, simple evaluation tool. See which Achiever Traits you need to become better at. Invest some time in them.

Rate yourself on a scale of 1 to 4:
1 = Strongly Disagree, 2 = Disagree, 3 = Agree, 4 = Strongly Agree

Achiever Trait	Personal Life	Professional Life
1. Ask Yourself Questions I am not afraid to ask myself the hard questions around what I am doing and whether it is meaningful to me.	1 2 3 4	1 2 3 4
Actions to Improve		
I take the time to listen honestly to my answers and act on them.	1 2 3 4	1 2 3 4
Actions to Improve		
2. Expand Your Perspective I purposefully consider how I might have "selective awareness" in any given situation.	1 2 3 4	1 2 3 4
Actions to Improve		
I consider new ways of looking at a situation so I don't limit my access to potential solutions.	1 2 3 4	1 2 3 4
Actions to Improve		

ACHIEVERS

Achiever Trait		Personal Life	Professional Life
3. Make a Plan I am clear on what I want to achieve, identifying my win.		1 2 3 4	1 2 3 4
Actions to Improve			
I have a step-by-step plan for how I will get there.		1 2 3 4	1 2 3 4
Actions to Improve			
4. Act Effectively I evaluate my actions regularly in terms of how it relates to reaching my win.		1 2 3 4	1 2 3 4
Actions to Improve			
I make changes and revisions when necessary to allow me to be more effective.		1 2 3 4	1 2 3 4
Actions to Improve			

Achiever Trait	Personal Life	Professional Life
5. Go the Distance When faced with a setback or a very difficult task, I don't give up easily.	1 2 3 4	1 2 3 4
Actions to Improve		
I like to pay attention to the details, leaving no stone unturned.	1 2 3 4	1 2 3 4
Actions to Improve		
6. Be Innovative I am open to new, different, and better ways of doing things.	1 2 3 4	1 2 3 4
Actions to Improve		
I will take a risk and get out of my comfort zone if I think it could lead to a better way of doing something.	1 2 3 4	1 2 3 4
Actions to Improve		

Achiever Trait	Personal Life	Professional Life
7. Utilize Power of Thought I consciously spend time considering what thoughts are going through my head and whether they are limiting or empowering.	1 2 3 4	1 2 3 4
Actions to Improve		
I purposefully use my thinking/thoughts to move me closer to my win(s).	1 2 3 4	1 2 3 4
Actions to Improve		
8. Generate Enthusiasm My attitude creates a place where people like to be around me and support me in my endeavors.	1 2 3 4	1 2 3 4
Actions to Improve		
I am able to feed off the energy and enthusiasm of those around me.	1 2 3 4	1 2 3 4
Actions to Improve		

The Leader Traits

Creating Champion
Organizations and Teams

Each of the Leader Traits has a graphic icon highlighted in blue to help support the key ideas found within.

LEADERS

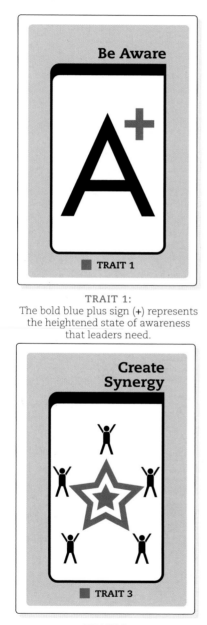

Be Aware

TRAIT 1

TRAIT 1:
The bold blue plus sign (+) represents the heightened state of awareness that leaders need.

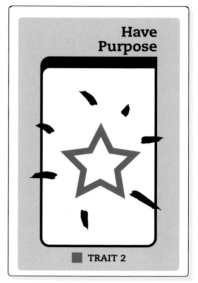

Have Purpose

TRAIT 2

TRAIT 2:
The large blue star represents a desired win to be held out for others.

Create Synergy

TRAIT 3

TRAIT 3:
The figures represent the team of people that success requires.

Show Conviction

TRAIT 4

TRAIT 4:
The blue heart represents the passion needed to lead others to overcome obstacles.

Use all eight icons as visual reminders of the key concepts and ideas within each of the Leader Traits.

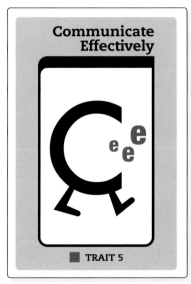

Communicate Effectively

TRAIT 5

TRAIT 5:
The walking C with the "e's" reminds us of the constant need for "e"ffective communication.

Exemplify Excellence

TRAIT 6

TRAIT 6:
The bold first figure shows us the example we set for others.

Embrace Contradictions

TRAIT 7

TRAIT 7:
The opposite expressions represent the contradictions we all face.

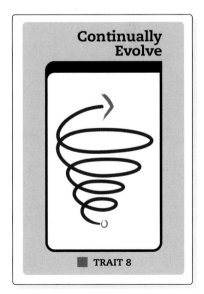

Continually Evolve

TRAIT 8

TRAIT 8:
The upward spiral represents the need to constantly grow.

I N THE LEADER TRAITS, we take the next step on the *Champion's Journey*. Leaders are very much champions in their own right, and their success shifts solely from themselves to depending upon how well they can help other people to reach their own wins.

What do we mean when we speak of leadership? We define leadership as the ability to create an environment where others can excel, where each person being led can bring out his or her strengths, and where many different individuals can contribute their personal best to the success of a team. This section outlines a set of eight fundamentals for leaders that provides a rock-solid foundation to make these things happen. These fundamentals enable you to create *winning* results for the organizations and teams you lead.

Many of us are leaders whether we realize it or not. Business people, such as CEOs, are leaders for certain, but so are coaches, parents, community activists, teachers, and many others who take on the roles and the responsibility of creating a winning environment for others.

Being a champion is one thing, but enabling others to become champions is something entirely different. It is not uncommon for people who excel as achievers to be promoted to a leadership position. But, just because you are a great achiever doesn't necessarily mean you have the skill sets to be a great leader.

What you will find within each Leader Trait in this section is a key concept that is the core learning. Each trait begins with a leadership anecdote from our own personal experience, followed by three supporting actions and short anecdotes that bring our ideas to life. At the end of each of the eight traits is a Review, which includes questions that engage you in self-reflection to make sure you are applying the trait. Once again, we have included an evaluation tool at the very end of the Leader section to help guide you in identifying where you might need to put your energy to get maximum results.

Applying these Leader Traits will help you connect others to their wins, and to create champion organizations and teams. Are you ready for the next set of traits on *The Champion's Journey*?

KEY CONCEPT
The greater your awareness, the greater your capacity to act effectively as a leader.

DEBBIE: I clearly remember early in my career, close to 30 years ago, when I led my team to a breakthrough success for the first time. We had won every event at the national championships. It was an amazing feat. Everyone kept commenting on how well we were positioned for a repeat at the next year's world championship trials. We were a shoe-in. Which was exactly when my fear and doubt set in.

On the surface, everything seemed fine. I'd faithfully show up at work every day, well prepared. But inside I was consumed with negative thinking and self-doubt. For the entire year, I kept asking myself, "How could we possibly repeat that success?" Suddenly, the stakes seemed so much higher, the pressure enormous. I worried about how embarrassed and humiliated I'd be when we failed to repeat our success. I thought about how badly I'd feel for the athletes when they didn't do as well as expected. I never made the connection between my thinking and my coaching performance.

Did we lose? You bet we did!

Initially, I blamed the judges. The beauty of being in a subjective sport is that you can always blame it on the judges! But in the end, I had to face the truth: Most of the blame lay with me. My negative thoughts were a major reason we had lost. So why didn't I just change my thinking? I couldn't. I wasn't even aware of what was going on in my head until it was all over.

Had I been more aware during that fateful year, I could have found ways to reframe the fear and worry, to change my thinking to be more empowering, which, in turn, would have improved my ability to connect the athletes to their full potential. Instead, I found myself getting angry easily during training, taking out my fear of failing on the athletes. I would berate *them* for making mistakes. I constantly focused on how bad things looked and how we would never win if we were swimming like this. Everything the athletes did just reinforced my mindset that we were going to lose.

My behavior had a profound impact on the day-to-day performance of the swimmers. More than ever before, they were continually calling in sick. And that only made my fear and panic worse. In turn, that weakened the athletes' performances. It became a self-fulfilling prophecy. Because of my lack of awareness, I could see very few possibilities for making the situation better. In my mind, I couldn't see us winning. I was overwhelmed with fear, which limited my approach the entire year. Negative thinking led to bad decisions and subsequent actions, which led to disappointing results. It was a very tough lesson to learn.

BEING A GREAT LEADER MEANS:
1. Being Aware Starts with You
2. Paying Attention to Others
3. Influencing What Is Happening Around You

1. Being Aware Starts with You

Leadership starts by increasing your internal awareness. What does being internally aware mean? It means simply that we are cognizant of what we are thinking, and then we make the connections between our thoughts and actions and how that influences not only ourselves, but also the people around us.

This takes us right back to the ideas explored in Achiever Trait 7, Utilize Power of Thought. There we learned how to tap into our sub-conscious thinking to become aware of how our thoughts impact our actions, and ultimately our results. As a leader, we build on this idea so that we become aware of not only how our thoughts affect ourselves, but how they affect those we are leading. Here is how it works:

The Awareness Cycle

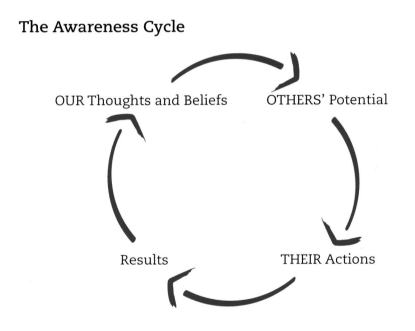

OUR Thoughts and Beliefs   OTHERS' Potential

Results   THEIR Actions

As a leader, the focus shifts to being aware of how our thoughts, beliefs, and actions can influence others. The Awareness Cycle simply reminds us to do the following:

1) Help others become aware of their own thinking.
2) Find the most effective way to positively impact others' thoughts to help them access their full potential.

In Debbie's story, it is pretty clear that she had no awareness of what she was thinking or how her negative mindset was influencing the team she was leading. Had she been more aware of her thoughts and their impact on those around her, she could have altered them to be more productive. As leaders, we can make changes before it is too late, consciously deciding what to think or what actions to take to be much more effective. A simple way to tap into this is to ask yourself some key questions:

- What am I thinking about in this situation?
- Is there any fear or worry attached to my thinking? If so, what is it?
- How can I make sure I do not pass this fear on to others by reframing any limiting thinking that may be present?

A mistake some leaders make is that they let their own issues of doubt or fear get in the way of leading others. They project or take things personally and often don't even realize they are doing it. This is why being aware starts with us. The great news here is that simply by becoming aware of something, we may be able to change it. Awareness is curative. Becoming aware of what needs to be changed is usually in itself enough to make the shift. At the very least, once something is brought to the surface of our consciousness, we can do something about it.

2. Paying Attention to Others

Once we are aware of what is going on with our own thoughts, we can then focus on enhancing our external awareness. What do we mean by being externally aware? We become aware of the thoughts and actions of others. It is external because heightened awareness enables us to get out of our heads and pay attention to what is going on with the people we are leading. Great leaders enable those they lead to develop their own skills, including building their own self-awareness.

MARK: *Good leaders can have a major impact on those they are leading simply by helping them become more aware of themselves. Many years ago, I was at a practice in the middle of a heavy training period and was poisoning the team with my negativity. I was being sarcastic, pulling a face as each instruction was given to us, bad-mouthing the coach behind his back. I was completely unaware of how I was single-handedly bringing down the entire group until the coach pulled me aside and pointed out what a negative impact I was having. He asked me what was going on, and helped me become aware of what I was thinking and feeling, and how that was translating into my actions. I knew from then on that whenever I was feeling tired, I had to be really careful that my tiredness didn't translate into negativity.*

The leader's role is to help others become more aware. Notice what is happening with the people you are leading. When things are working, make sure you tell them so they become aware and continue to do the right things, and even make them better. And when things aren't working, make sure to point that out as well so people become aware of what they need to change.

3. Influencing What is Happening Around You

You must pay attention to your immediate environment, as well as be aware of how larger events might have an impact on your day-to-day reality. We do not live or work in silos. Notice what you notice. Pay attention to what is going on around you daily, as well as to those things in the bigger picture that might ultimately impact your final results. Understand how outside forces can potentially determine your outcome. With this awareness, you have access to more choices, possibilities, and solutions for yourself and others.

LEADERS

DEBBIE: In the four years leading up to the Sydney Olympics, I worked with the Australian synchronized swimming team. They were ranked last in the world, and I had the challenge of getting them to place in the top eight. Each year, our routines and technical skill improved dramatically, but each year we would come back with the same result, the bottom of the pack. Even though we became much better than other countries, we just couldn't move ahead. I couldn't figure out what was wrong. It was very frustrating.

Eventually, in one of those "ah-ha!" moments, it came to me. I blamed the judges again, but this time with reason. It was the judges' selective awareness that was not allowing them to see how good we were really getting. In order to justify placing us at the bottom, where they were used to seeing us, the judges were only noticing the things we were doing wrong and not what we were doing right. When these same judges marked the top teams, they took the opposite approach, noticing only what they liked so they could justify putting them in the top half of the field. Coming from a country that was always in the medals, I had never been aware of this phenomenon, and why would I as long as we were winning. How could I lead these judges to look at us in a different light?

At the next competition, I asked a couple of judges what they noticed that the Australians were doing right. As expected, they had no answers. But it shifted their awareness so that the next time they judged us, they started to look at what was working, largely because they knew I would come and ask them. This was the turning point for us. They started to notice what we were doing well and our marks went up accordingly. Eventually, we made it into the finals at the World Championships and top eight at the Olympics, a first for Australia in front of their hometown crowd at the 2000 Sydney Games.

■ TRAIT 1 REVIEW: Be Aware

BEING A GREAT LEADER MEANS:
1. Being Aware Starts with You
2. Paying Attention to Others.
3. Influencing What is Happening Around You

KEY CONCEPT
The greater your awareness, the greater your capacity to act effectively as a leader.

REALITY CHECK!
As leaders, it is easy to fall into a state of unawareness as we go through our day-to-day routine. We need to know what is going on with those we are leading. We must understand the environment around us. And that starts by being aware of ourselves. If we are projecting our own insecurities onto those we are leading, we hold them back. By keeping our awareness levels high, we get ourselves out of the way in order to connect to those around us and focus on the job at hand.

Bring This Trait to Life
As different situations unfold, check in with yourself:
1. Are you aware of your own thoughts, actions, and their impact?
2. Are you paying attention to the thoughts and actions of others?
3. Are you creating the circumstances for yourself and others to achieve champion results?

LEADERS

TRAIT 2:
Have Purpose

KEY CONCEPT
By capturing people's imagination with a clear objective, you inspire every individual to do their part in making it happen.

MARK: *At my first Olympic Games in Seoul in 1988, I had placed fifth in my individual event, which had been enormously disappointing because I was nowhere near my personal best. I was actually a full second off. But I was given another chance at winning a medal the next day, as part of a relay team. Not that I ever thought that was going to happen. The four of us on that team had placed anywhere from fourth to tenth in our individual events, and just getting through to the final seemed like a reasonable expectation. But one of the team members was anything but reasonable.*

Victor Davis was a swimming legend, partly for his accomplishments, but as much for his behavior. He was as famous for breaking world records and being a world champion as he was for kicking a chair halfway across the pool in front of the Queen of England following a disqualification. He was a competitor. But he was 24, which was old for a swimmer at that time, and this relay would be his last chance at an Olympic medal, so he took the lead that day.

83

The morning of the event, Victor came to us, his three teammates, and rallied us around a common purpose. He thought we could surprise everyone and win the silver medal. He clearly explained what we would each need to do to make that happen. As he spoke, the other two of my teammates started to share in his vision. They could see it, too. Unfortunately, I couldn't. Having had a disappointment less than 24 hours earlier, I wasn't able to immediately let myself dream of winning a medal. I protected myself, remaining standoffish.

A number of hours before the race, Victor approached me. An imposing man at 6'3", he was very intimidating. He put his arm around my shoulders and looked me straight in the eyes and asked, "Tewksbury, when you were a kid, what did you dream of?" I replied, "I dreamed of winning a medal at the Olympics. Unfortunately, it didn't happen." To which he responded, "You better wake up. You have two guys over there and me who want more than anything to win a medal. But we can't do it without you. It is there for us to take, but only if you are with us. All I am asking is for you to do your part. But I leave it up to you." Then he walked away. By inviting me to share in his purpose, he broke through my resistance and made it clear what was expected of me.

For the rest of the day, we hung out together as a team. Victor checked in with me constantly to see if I was all right, if everything was on track. He kept asking my teammates and me over and over again if we could see the medal. By the time the race came that night, we knew what we needed to do. We would shock everyone in the pool on that last evening of the swimming competition by shattering the national record and winning the Olympic silver medal.

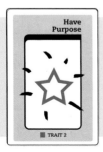

BEING A GREAT LEADER MEANS:
1. Setting a Compelling Vision
2. Planning to Bring the Vision to Life
3. Keeping Everyone on Track

1. Setting a Compelling Vision

Make it clear why everyone is there. In Achiever Trait 3, Make a Plan, we looked at the importance of planning, which started by specifically identifying an objective. The same idea holds true for having purpose: part of what this means *is* planning, but this time, as a leader, the objective you identify is more global in scope because it involves something for yourself and others to achieve.

Great leadership requires setting a vision that acts as the guiding force, and has a sense of awe and possibility. When you identify a clear, compelling challenge, people get excited and rise to meet it. Capturing everyone's imagination through a common purpose is difficult, but it is also extremely powerful. In order for that to happen, you need to figure out what you really want to accomplish, and what people will collectively commit to achieve.

When people share a sense of purpose with each other, even the most challenging hurdles can be overcome. Often, though, we don't take the time to clarify our purpose with those we are leading; we just assume people know why they are there.

DEBBIE: A few years ago, I worked with two companies that were in the web design industry but who approached their businesses completely differently. Company 1 laid out a very clear, specific purpose that was quite ambitious, and it got everyone within the company excited. Their vision was to develop award-winning international websites for global companies. From that ultimate dream, each department knew what their overriding objective was.

In contrast, Company 2 lacked a clear purpose, and was never willing to work seriously at changing that. They set a broad goal of designing websites for people. But no one knew exactly where to start. For example, when the marketing department staff tried to develop their action plan, they had no focus. They didn't know what specifically they were trying to do, other than to find people who wanted websites. They had no idea how to target a market, or identify who their clients would be.

Within two years, Company 1 had surpassed all business expectations, both in terms of industry recognition and revenues. Company 2 never really committed to working together, and sadly closed their doors within a year. Setting a compelling vision that people can rally around and that gives everyone their own sense of purpose is fundamental to success.

2. Planning to Bring the Vision to Life

Okay, so we've got the big picture. Now, everyone needs to embrace and feel a part of that vision in his or her own way. This happens when people are clear about exactly what is expected of them, and they are equally clear about how their individual role connects back to the overall objective. This is the distinction of planning as a leader as opposed to planning as an achiever. We are no longer creating a road map just for ourselves; we are creating a strategic plan in consultation with others to ensure that all of the individual parts lead to realizing the vision.

Essentially, the plan connects each person to her or his individual role. The more specific we can be about each person's role and the clearer our intentions are for their outcomes, the more likely they are to happen.

Now, here is the catch. The leader makes sure people know what the objective is and what is expected of them, but how they get there becomes each person's job. When they are given this responsibility, people take ownership of the overall purpose and their role in making it happen. They become empowered and self-motivated, and hold themselves accountable to get their piece of the whole done as best as they can. If not personally engaged, then why would they care if they did it well or not?

MARK: *I spoke recently to an organization that had an ambitious vision of delivering the most spectacular travel experience in the world. Great. But within that, the leaders' challenge was to have the thousand-plus employees plan how they were going to bring that vision to life for themselves. They did that by having each person consider how they would fill in the following blank: "I am going to bring spectacular to life by _____." People took it and ran with it, carrying a card on them at work that reminded them everyday of what their personal* objective was. *"I will provide spectacular service, or spectacular greetings, or spectacular safety." This simple exercise made it clear to each individual within the organization his or her role in bringing the larger organizational purpose to life. And it solidified this company's position as one of the best high-end travel providers in the world.*

3. Keeping Everyone on Track

Some leaders worry that if they allow people to do things their own way, they then lose control and chaos follows. A clear purpose is what keeps people on track, becoming the measuring stick by which everyone can assess their actions. Similar to making a plan as an achiever, once you know where you want to go, you work backwards with people to develop clear performance indicators and targets directly related to the overall objective. As a result, individuals can tell how well they are doing along the way. Here are some questions that will guide you in the process:

∎ What is the overall objective and what do we need to do in order to reach that?
∎ Are we busy doing the right things or are we just busy doing things?
∎ How will we know if we are being successful on a daily basis?

Great leaders constantly evaluate how people are doing, and if they are on track to meet their established benchmarks. How your team gets there is their business. *If* they get there is your business.

Essentially, our role as the leader is to ensure that everyone is effectively doing their part to bring the overall vision to life. With a great strategic plan in place, instead of being at the mercy of unfolding events, we remain focused but fluid, able to revise as necessary. Rather than being married blindly to the strategic plan, the leader is able to find alternative and more effective routes for individuals to achieve the overall purpose when necessary. The ideas in this trait (Have Purpose) sound very straightforward, but this is where so many leaders end up failing. Holding out a clear vision and keeping people, including yourself, on track is what great leaders do.

LEADERS

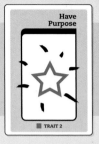

■ TRAIT 2 REVIEW: Have Purpose

BEING A GREAT LEADER MEANS:
1. Setting a Compelling Vision
2. Planning to Bring the Vision to Life
3. Keeping Everyone on Track

KEY CONCEPT
By capturing people's imagination with a clear objective, you inspire every individual to do their part in making it happen.

REALITY CHECK!
It is ironic that what we often stray furthest from as leaders is our purpose. Many of us simply get caught in reactionary mode. As distraction after distraction come hurling toward us, we often forget to see how our decisions actually connect back to that original raison d'être. We had a purpose, but since we strayed from it and aren't acting effectively, then what is the point? Really keeping the purpose in mind gives clarity and guides decision making, helping keep us and those we lead on track.

Bring This Trait to Life
As different situations unfold, check in with yourself:
1. Have you set a compelling vision?
2. Are people clear on their role in achieving that vision?
3. Have you established clear targets and benchmarks to measure progress along the way?

LEADERS

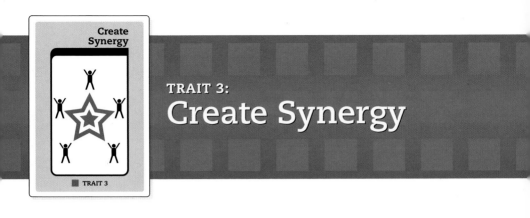

Create Synergy

KEY CONCEPT

By bringing together the right people, an inexplicable energy is created that produces winning results much greater than any one individual's contribution.

DEBBIE: After the Los Angeles Olympics, I wasn't satisfied with winning two silver medals. It was hard to settle for second when I knew we had the potential to win. In reflecting back, I realized that one of the reasons we hadn't won gold was because I had wanted to do it all by myself. I thought I didn't need any help. Unfortunately, I had been driven from a place of ego, and I didn't want to share the journey or the glory with anyone else. Thankfully, I realized that if we were going to be successful at the next Olympics, I couldn't do it all alone. To be the best, I needed to build a support team of experts around me.

One of our goals was to be physiologically better than we had ever been before, doing things with a higher degree of difficulty than anyone in the world had seen. But I didn't know how to train this. I had heard about Dr. David Smith, also known as Doctor Death, an exercise physiologist renowned for his intense, difficult testing programs. In Dr. Smith, I found the right person to take care of the first challenge of getting us physiologically excellent.

A fundamental part of our success would be determined by how we were judged. Although this was out of my control, I wanted to do what I could to make the international judges a part of our journey. Working with Synchro Canada, our national organization, we held a seminar where we used the opportunity to showcase our Olympic athletes so that we could get input from the judges on what they liked and how they would respond to certain parts of the routine. This was a bit unconventional, and strange as it may sound, these judges became a part of our support team.

One of my greatest lessons from my first Olympics was how important the hometown advantage had been for the Americans. I wanted to find ways to connect with a Korean audience as though we were the hometown favorites. A Korean/Canadian woman, Mrs. Chang, filled this role perfectly for us. She had been an interpreter for a visiting Korean national team at the Pan Pacific Championships earlier that year in Calgary. She took us to Korea in March of the Olympic year and was a gem because she was connected to so many important people in Korea. We did water shows, gave clinics with the up-and-coming Korean national team athletes, visited schools, and received media attention. The Koreans were working to build their program, and it was a great exchange. All of these actions built relationships so that when we came back to the Olympics, the Koreans remembered and supported us.

The two gold medals we won would have never been possible without the extended team's support over the years. It had been a collective effort of these people and so many more that made us champions. Each person had their own area of expertise, with clear ideas about how they were going to do their part. Everyone, from Dr. Smith to the judges, to Mrs. Chang and beyond, took pride in their particular role in making the overall objective of winning the Olympics a reality.

BEING A GREAT LEADER MEANS:
1. Getting the Right People in the Right Roles
2. Guiding the Group to Gel as a High-Performing Team
3. Finding Ways to Keep the Team Performing at Its Best

1. Getting the Right People in the Right Roles

Being a great leader doesn't mean that you are the best at everything. It means that you are great at identifying what roles you need filled, and who are the best people to fill them. Done well, you can get out of the way and let those around you do what they do best.

When creating a team, every individual has a clear primary role that draws upon their expertise. At any one time, any person on the team might take the lead depending on the task at hand. Every person's ability to operate at a world-class level in their particular role gives the group added confidence in its ability to achieve the collective objectives. As the group shares progress, victories, and setbacks, the synergy starts to kick in. But synergy also comes from more than just that.

In reality, the power of a high-functioning team goes well beyond the official titles and identified roles of the people within the group. Every person on the team will bring their own unique style and personality to the table. We call this an individual's X Factor, that unquantifiable energy that she or he brings to the group. Extremely difficult to measure, if not impossible, this combination of skill *and* personality often creates the magic that makes teams work. It is the combination of the right people in the right roles along with the X Factor that creates the synergy where 2 + 2 equals much, much more than 4.

LEADERS

2. Guiding the Group to Gel as a High-Performing Team

Synergy doesn't just happen. It is the outcome of a carefully guided process. As leaders, we have to understand the dynamic phases through which teams form. A couple of skills are required to do this. First, you need to call upon the awareness you developed in the first leadership trait to identify which phase your team is at. Then, if they are not at a high-performing level, you need to be able to move them through the various phases to get there. From our experience (and adapted from team-building theory), we have identified and given a brief description of the five dynamic phases involved in building teams.

The Five Dynamic Phases in Team Building

■ Dynamic Phase 1: Meet and Greet
You come together as a team and meet each other. Everyone is on guard, polite but cautious. If the team is doing well, it is because people are doing their individual parts effectively. It will take some time to become consistently effective as a team.

■ Dynamic Phase 2: True Colors
The team gets to know each other. Relationships begin to form. Cliques and alliances might emerge. Some confrontation and arguments might unfold. Generally, the team members are not committed to the collective purpose or to each other yet, remaining more focused mainly on themselves and their own individual tasks.

■ Dynamic Phase 3: Clicking Together
A process is formed around how to work together. The group begins making decisions and finding solutions. People become committed to the collective objective, and at the same time, evaluate their own effectiveness.

■ Dynamic Phase 4: High Performance
The team is firing on all cylinders. It is completing its work efficiently, effectively, and seemingly effortlessly. People feel confident and supported, and are open to each other's ideas. Roles are clear, and real progress is made. There is an excitement to push the bar higher, every-

one feeding off the collective momentum of the group. There is an underlying resourcefulness, flexibility, and joy in working together.

■ Dynamic Phase 5: Declining Performance
The team becomes self-satisfied, complacent, and bored. Self-interest is evident; ideas are no longer challenged as patterns set in. Criticism is seen as disloyalty and may be followed by isolation or rejection. The team enters into a period of decline.

MARK: *Following my athletic career, I joined the International Olympic Committee as part of the site selection commission. Basically, 15 of us from different parts of the world and backgrounds came together to create a team whose purpose was to evaluate the bids from the 11 cities vying to host the 2004 Olympics. Each member was chosen for their particular expertise—myself as the athlete, someone else for security, another for the environment, and so on. It was a very challenging experience because our mission was only going to take three months, so we had to gel as a team very quickly.*

At our first stop, each of us performed well in our own area of expertise, but in isolation from each other. In the second city, two of our members were at each other's throats. By the third city, we had overcome the initial hostility and awkwardness, gotten to know each other, and had found the best ways to work together. By the fourth city, we had hit our stride, effortlessly and quickly evaluating whether a city was right to host the Games or not. It didn't take long for the team to form, largely because we were all allowed to take a leadership role within our own area of expertise.

The challenge was that almost as quickly as we had gelled, we got complacent. We stayed in the high-performance mode for four or five cities, but then we started to get bored, returned to fighting with each other, and individuals started to feel ostracized. The head of the commission wasn't aware of the team dynamics because his political interests eventually prevailed over the needs of the team. By the time we arrived in our final cities, we were in decline, interfering with each other's respective roles, and no longer honoring the high-functioning group we had once been.

LEADERS

3. Finding Ways to Keep the Team Performing at its Best

Great leaders get the group into the high-performance phase and keep them there as much as possible. Teams tend to move in and out of the various phases, which is why we call them dynamic. The challenge is to effectively get the best out of each person within the team.

Bringing a group of people together to perform at their highest levels is not easy. Within any given team, there may be strong personalities that don't see eye-to-eye. This is not a bad thing. It can even be an advantage when differences of opinion are nurtured and the team looks at things from different perspectives. The leader's job is like that of a symphony conductor, getting each person to play their role and, at the same time, complement one another. This skill is where leaders need to pay a lot of attention.

Where some leaders make a mistake is in trying to crush or silence differences of opinion, imposing their own opinions instead, often to the exclusion of others. This, in effect, undermines the confidence of team members. Leaders help to kill the synergy and move a team away from the high-performance phase when they do the following:

- micromanage
- interfere unnecessarily
- take away responsibility
- over-control
- don't share information with the group
- make it about themselves
- become inflexible and lose their temper

When they do these things, they block the energy of the group. Their behavior creates distrust, and a toxic environment results that will breed mediocrity.

The other extreme is equally as dangerous, when leaders do the following:

- don't have an opinion
- never intervene
- allow others to completely take over
- are overly flexible
- don't speak out when things aren't right

Then the team cannot perform at its highest level either because there is no one guiding the process. Mediocrity also thrives in this circumstance.

We know we are focusing on the negative here. Unfortunately, so many of us have had this kind of experience when being led, or might even see ourselves demonstrating some of these characteristics listed above. To put it more positively, as leaders, when we entrust the right people to focus on doing what they do well and give them the space and tools to do it, guiding the process when necessary but not interfering needlessly, the team flourishes. At the end of the day, it is important to remember that creating synergy is not about you as a leader; it is about bringing out the best in others. Of course, this process cannot happen without you. Finding that careful balance to let people do what they do well and reigning in the team when needed in order to keep functioning at the highest possible level is what great leaders know how to do.

DEBBIE: Because of my experience in developing Olympic and world champions, I was part of a group brought together to work with many different sports within the national sport system. Our purpose was to help them create the environment necessary for their athletes to achieve high levels of performance. In this job, I was joined by several world-class experts, all of us excited to be working together toward a common goal. But what should have been a dream experience turned into a nightmare.

It came down to the leader of the project. He thought his CEO title meant that he was supposed to not only tell everyone what the objective was, but how to do their individual roles as well. From his perspective, all of his experts were simply there to do what he told them to do. Great leaders would have seen this as an opportunity to create a team of world-class experts whose collective knowledge would be unmatched. Unfortunately, this leader had no idea how to bring the best out of people and capitalize on the strength of his team. Slowly, the environment turned sour and unproductive.

As we tried to explain to him why some of the things he was making us do were not the best way to go, he simply became angry and even more dictatorial. Roles and responsibilities that had been assigned were suddenly taken away. The group started to become cynical, feeling defeated and utterly useless as they tried to make things work, but were instead kept busier and busier doing things that had nothing to do with reaching the common goal. Ultimately, the team fell apart. The boss stayed, but everyone else moved on.

■ TRAIT 3 REVIEW: Create Synergy

BEING A GREAT LEADER MEANS:
1. Getting the Right People in the Right Roles
2. Guiding the Group to Gel as a High-Performing Team
3. Finding Ways to Keep the Team Performing at Its Best

KEY CONCEPT
By bringing together the right people, an inexplicable energy is created that produces winning results much greater than any one individual's contribution.

REALITY CHECK!
Where leaders fall down is often twofold. First, they don't get the best people in the identified roles. Second, they don't let people do their jobs. It is hard to let go of the idea that you don't have to do it all by yourself. If you don't allow people to do what they do best, then you are going to compromise overall performance. When you create synergy, you have a team of people who are individually great at what they do, and together are even greater.

Bring This Trait to Life
As different situations unfold, check in with yourself:
1. Are you getting the right people in the right roles in order to fulfill a specific purpose?
2. Are you guiding those individual experts to work well together?
3. Is a high-performing, synergetic team of champions being created?

LEADERS

TRAIT 4:
Show Conviction

KEY CONCEPT

By being passionate and believing completely in what you
are doing, it enables you and the people you lead to break
through enormous obstacles.

MARK: *In 2001, I was part of a team from Montreal that won the right
to host a major international event, The Gay Games. It was to be the
largest in the movement's history, with an expected 16,000 participants.
Along with sport and culture, for the first time ever in sport history,
including the Olympic Games, we were organizing an internationally
recognized human rights conference that would be opened by the United
Nations High Commissioner. It would be a spectacular gathering. But
then disaster struck. After two years of negotiating, we failed to come to
an agreement with the governing body of the event. Halfway to delivering the Games, we had them stripped from us. Needless to say, we found
ourselves in a most difficult situation.*

*In regrouping, we came to many realizations. We had a clear vision
for what this event could be. We had a solid plan to make it happen. All
of our financial partners agreed to stay with us if we decided to go*

ahead with games under a different name. Even though the challenge was enormous and there were many times when it would have been easy to give up, we had an undying belief in what we were doing. So we created a new event. Personally, I was convinced that within the gay sport movement something had to change, and that we were the right group of people in the right city to make it happen. But unless the participants came, all of this was for nothing. And in order to get them onside, we had to win their trust and confidence.

On a snowy, blizzard weekend in January, we invited sport leaders from around the world to join us in Montreal to explain what had happened when we lost the Gay Games, and to look forward toward the future. There were representatives from Australia, the United States, Canada, Germany, Denmark, and South America. The mood was challenging, with many people unclear about what had really happened in the negotiating process, and doubtful whether they should support us in Montreal. After two days of meetings, it came down to a moment when a decision would have to be made. With this group's support, we could have our Games; without it, we were finished.

I was the person who had to make that final pitch. As I passionately shared our vision for the future, I explained how we had arrived at this moment, and then asked the leaders if they believed a new organization was necessary to move forward. One by one the leaders stood and said the old way wasn't working. We voted unanimously to start something new.

BEING A GREAT LEADER MEANS:
1. Believing Completely in What You Are Doing
2. Getting Through the Tough Times
3. Strengthening Confidence in Others

1. Believing Completely in What You Are Doing

Of all the leadership traits, this one is perhaps the most difficult to articulate, because it represents the essence of a leader, the spirit in which someone embodies leadership. Think about it. When someone believes completely in what they are doing, it is obvious, compelling, and magnetic. We can't help but be drawn to them, or at the very least respect their passion. It is why conviction is so fundamental to leaders. Would you really want to follow someone who doesn't believe completely in what they are doing?

That is not to say that as a leader we don't have self-doubt and moments of questioning. Great leaders are competent because from time to time they have feelings of incompetence, which forces them to reconnect with what it is they believe in. Upon reflection, they then have a renewed sense of conviction, knowing clearly why they are doing what they are doing, and why they believed so strongly in it in the first place. Incompetent leaders, on the other hand, often don't take the time to stop and ask themselves questions. They mistake their busyness for competence, but when they really get tested, they often don't have the true belief to see things through.

DEBBIE: For the past three years, I have worked with several national team coaches from different sports. My role was advising them on how to improve their on-the-job performance. It was in the way that the coaches spoke about their teams that gave away their level of conviction to me. What I noticed was that whenever their teams or athletes had success, many of the coaches would talk from the "we" perspective. "*We* rose to the challenge today" or "*We* put in the hard work." Whenever they had disappointing results, all of a sudden the talk became about "they." "*They* underperformed" or "*They* got complacent and lazy out there." The coaches weren't taking responsibility for the team when it wasn't doing well. Who is going to give it all for someone who in the heat of the battle turns from *we* to *they*?

From the team's point of view, the coaches believed in them only when they were succeeding. If they weren't winning, the coaches lost confidence and didn't have faith in them anymore. When this was brought to the coaches' attention, it allowed them to see how their conviction appeared to be wavering when times got tough. It forced them to go back and really ask themselves if they believed in the team or not. If you find your conviction is wavering, it forces you to reevaluate. Is there something you need to do to get that conviction back? The coaches had to find ways to show that conviction in the hard times as well as in the good times.

2. Getting Through the Tough Times

Regardless of who we are leading and what objective we are leading them to, there will most certainly be times that are incredibly challenging. It is an inevitable part of leadership. It is our conviction that drives our actions, enabling us *and* the people we are leading to break through challenges. We must never underestimate the power of conviction.

Conviction drives our actions and enables others to follow. This is the trait that gives you the determination to succeed against all odds. It is a force deep in your gut, a knowing that you just have to do what you have to do. Conviction enables us to bounce back when things don't work out. In fact, a great way to measure the strength of your conviction is by seeing whether you are able to come back after failure.

MARK: *One of the legends of my sport was a Soviet swimmer named Vladimir Salnikov. He burst onto the international scene as a 16-year-old finalist at the 1976 Olympics in the 1500 meter freestyle, the marathon of swimming. In the years following those Olympics, Vladimir dominated his event, and was all set to win gold in front of a hometown crowd at the 1980 Moscow Olympics four years later. Although he became an Olympic champion, the western countries had boycotted the Games, and the win seemed empty. So Vladimir kept swimming for four more years. Still at the top of the world rankings, a remarkable feat in itself, he was prepared to defend his title at the 1984*

Los Angeles Olympics. Two months before the Games were to begin, the eastern bloc countries of the world boycotted, and Salnikov never got his chance.

Vladimir decided to keep swimming following the boycott, wanting to win an Olympic gold medal when the entire world was there. In 1986, though, he didn't make the final at the World Championships. As he prepared for the 1988 Seoul Olympics, everyone gave up on him. At 28 years old, the world agreed that his dream was impossible. So what did he do? Vladimir fired all of his coaches, took the reins, and built a team around himself that he led with his undying conviction. I was there when he touched the wall first and became the oldest gold medalist in our sport's history.

3. Strengthening Confidence in Others

It is important not to confuse conviction with bravado. When the going gets really tough and someone's belief is based on bravado and empty talk, it almost guarantees that the leader won't go the distance. Instead, they distance themselves and those they are leading from ever reaching the objective. There is no substance to support the words, and everything falls apart accordingly. Once leaders display this behavior, it is very difficult to regain a level of trust and confidence from those they are leading.

Conviction is based on a genuine belief. It solidifies confidence in the objective and people's ability to reach it. As a leader, your belief impacts not only your own actions, but also the thoughts, beliefs, and actions of those you are leading. When you have an unwavering resolve in yourself, in others, and in doing what needs to be done, individuals respond accordingly. Our conviction taps into others' potential, helping them to connect to stronger performances.

Simply put, when you are passionate and energized by what you are doing, it spreads. Your spirit ripples to others, giving them added confidence and strength as they strive to reach their full potential. Conviction is often that little extra that enables people to override their limiting beliefs and breaks them through to higher levels of performance.

LEADERS

DEBBIE: When I first started coaching, I was given all the hand-me-downs, the athletes the experienced coaches didn't want to coach because they weren't going to win anything. One of the swimmers I inherited had been labeled as a slow learner in school. Her mother made it a point to come and explain this to me. "Don't expect too much from her. We're just grateful you let her join the club."

As I was working with this girl, I realized that there was nothing to support this label. Yes, it may take her a while to get something, but once she got it, she really got it. I believed completely based on what I saw working with her that she had a rare talent and that she was a huge asset to any team. I shared this with her. "You know, you aren't a slow learner at all. You just take more time to learn something because once you have learned it, you never forget it."

This was a huge awakening for her. My genuine conviction in her ability translated to her believing that there was nothing wrong with how she learned, it was just different. She actually felt quite special, taking pride in the fact that once she had it, she retained it. This created a belief in her that made her a fierce competitor. She went on to win a bronze medal at the Junior National Championships, beating out all of her teammates—the ones who were supposedly much better.

■ TRAIT 4 REVIEW: Show Conviction

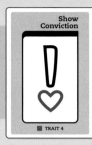

BEING A GREAT LEADER MEANS:
1 Believing Completely in What You Are Doing
2. Getting Through the Tough Times
3. Strengthening Confidence in Others

KEY CONCEPT
By being passionate and believing completely in what you are doing, it enables you and the people you lead to break through enormous obstacles.

REALITY CHECK!
Often as leaders we face really tough times en route to where we want to go. To get through, we are asked to believe not only for ourselves, but for others as well. And you just can't fake it. Conviction is real; people can feel it, and when you are honest with them and show what you believe, they rally then, too. It doesn't mean that there aren't moments of self-doubt. There are. But when you don't give up, when you commit and lead through the tough times by showing conviction, it helps others through as well.

Bring This Trait to Life
As different situations unfold, check in with yourself:
1. Are you connected to that infectious passion that ensures you never give up on yourself?
2. Do you overcome setbacks, and enable those you are leading to overcome moments of doubt?
3. Does your conviction inspire others?

LEADERS

TRAIT 5:
Communicate Effectively

KEY CONCEPT
By creating an open environment where ideas can be exchanged freely, people are clear and engaged in the process.

DEBBIE: I was brought in to work on communication skills with Peter, the director of software development in a large web design company. He had alienated many people, one of his project managers going so far as to threaten to quit if she had to work with him anymore.

Peter explained how sometimes after just one conversation, people seemed to shut him out. He gave me an example. "I had been discussing some work that had been done for a client with an account manager. I told him that I couldn't believe the lack of quality in the work that had been done to date. It was obvious someone hadn't been doing his or her job. That had been when the conversation halted, and after that our relationship hadn't been the same."

I asked Peter if he thought perhaps the account manager had taken what he said personally. "Maybe he felt what you said was slamming him for not paying attention to the quality of the work?" A little light went on in Peter's head. He said he'd never meant it like that, but he saw how it could be taken that way.

A few weeks later, we were having one of our regular coaching meetings and Peter said he'd blown it again. Another manager had asked him to review a particular project they had been working on to give her some feedback. He didn't like what he saw and sent her an e-mail telling her how bad it was and embarrassing for the company to produce something of such poor quality. Needless to say, this was not the most effective approach. At least Peter realized this. However, he didn't know how to say it any differently. Since he was trying to build a good working relationship with this person, he really needed to figure it out. He asked how he might have expressed himself in another way, especially since he didn't want to lie about what he really thought.

I suggested one solution might be to say, "I can see lots of opportunity for making this site a lot better." What the person hears is "opportunity" and "better" as opposed to "this is an embarrassment to the company." It opens up the possibilities instead of restricting them. There is a huge difference. Peter came to realize that communication was not just about getting the point across, it was equally important to understand how that message was received.

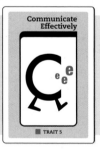

BEING A GREAT LEADER MEANS:
1. Paying Attention to the Words You Use
2. Noticing the Response You Get
3. Keeping Communication Flowing

1. Paying Attention to the Words You Use

Communication seems to be the ultimate buzzword within our society. Whenever there is a problem within an organization, often it is credited to a "lack of communication." But here is the deal. Often times, no one is really clear what that expression actually means. It seems the solution is to increase the *quantity* of communication without paying attention to the *quality*. We can send a multitude of memos, make endless phone calls, copy everyone on e-mails, send out newsletters, and have weekly meetings, and at the end of the day, we still might not have managed to communicate anything meaningful. If we haven't paid attention to the words we are using and how we get our message across, then what is the point?

Words are fundamental to effective communication. We use words to share purpose, articulate roles and responsibilities, express our feeling and emotions, share our knowledge, and to give instructions. But we use words so automatically that very little thought goes into *which* words we use, or *how* and *when* we use them. Words can pack a big punch. And often, without us realizing it, it is the words we use and how we use them that can *inhibit* or *maximize* performance. By becoming more aware of how we use words—both in spoken and written form—as well as our timing, we can more effectively help others access their full potential.

MARK: *A legendary communication disaster happened to one of the Olympic coaches who both Debbie and I know. In fact, Debbie was at a banquet when this national team coach confided in her that he was proud for having taken responsibility for his coaching mistakes. Admitting an error is honorable, but when you admit it is probably even more important. Like the famous expression, timing is everything.*

This particular coach recognized he had made a fundamental error in preparing his athletes to have their best performance at the Olympics. He mistimed the competition, realizing that his athletes would not be ready for the actual Games, but would peak one week later instead. And he felt sick about it. So what did he do? He sat his athletes down two nights before the Olympics began and apologized to them, wanting to let them know that he was taking the blame for the bad results that were about to happen when they competed. "I screwed up. You're not ready to race at your best. I am so sorry."

Not only was the timing of his message unbelievably bad, but the words he chose relayed the message that these athletes who had prepared their entire lives for this moment were not going to be ready to

LEADERS

race well, no matter what. And no surprise, they didn't. His words became a self-fulfilling prophecy.

Even if this coach had to tell them the "truth," he could have chosen his words differently so that he didn't close the door on possibility. The reality is that at an Olympics, many factors such as levels of adrenaline and degrees of preparation make it nearly impossible to predict what might happen on the actual day in any Olympic event. As good as it was to be able to admit making a mistake, the timing in this case was completely off. Who knows what might have happened if the coach hadn't said anything at all?

The point here is to be aware of the words we are using and the time at which we say them, understanding the impact they have on those we are leading. The wrong words at the wrong time limit possibilities; the right words at the right time expand them.

2. Noticing the Response You Get

Great leadership is about allowing information to flow both ways, not just about the leader issuing orders. A key function of leadership is to pay as much attention to the feedback we are receiving as we do to what we are saying in the first place.

Information comes to us in different ways. The actions of those we are leading give us insight into what they are thinking, and can show us what is or is not working. Their behavior is a good starting point to figure out what we need to know in order to see if they understood us. So is listening to the words they use, and what they are saying. Getting as much information back as possible, we can communicate with each individual more effectively, making sure they are connected to the objective. It is important to observe and listen carefully to what people are doing and telling us.

If what we are seeing and hearing isn't giving us enough information to clearly figure out what is going on, then we need to ask questions in order to get more information. How we frame our questions will directly influence the quality of the answers. A question has the power to shut a person down—*"What on earth were you thinking?"*—or open a person up—*"What results were you hoping to get?"*

If we are not getting the response that we are looking for, then it is important to change how we are communicating to a way that works for that person. Remember that the meaning of communication is the response we get. As a leader, it is ultimately your job to figure out how to get the point across. It doesn't mean that you are a dictator, or that you are there to tell people what to do. It means that when the people we are leading need something to help them improve, it is our responsibility to find the best possible way to get that message through to them.

DEBBIE: Over the years, as my athletes became more and more successful at the international level, other coaches would come and observe our training to see what it was we were doing that led to winning results. One particular coach from another sport made the comment that he was amazed at how much I let the swimmers talk back to me.

So what was I doing? I was simply asking them questions about how they felt something was working, and then listening to their responses. If they didn't think it was working, they felt safe enough to say so. For the other coach, this was seen as being disrespectful. He thought the athletes should just do what they're told. For me, getting feedback from them was absolutely crucial. At the end of the day, this wasn't about me or how much control I had. It was about finding the best solutions for the team. Without asking those critical questions, we would be settling for mediocrity.

Unfortunately, this is where many leaders run into challenges. There is a misplaced desire to tell people what to do without considering what is going on with them. Some leaders think that by yelling at people, telling them how to feel, or imposing their worldview and opinions on others that they are communicating. In effect, they are closing people down by being this way, eliminating the chance of information to flow and for both sides to get better.

LEADERS

3. Keeping Communication Flowing

When done well, effective communication means that our points get across in a timely fashion. Essentially, we are listening and observing, as well as giving and getting feedback to ensure that each person, including ourselves, is clear. Does everyone understand exactly what is expected of them and what is needed to do things even better? From this comes a by-product that is the magic of effective communication: an environment is created where everyone feels safe to communicate freely, to express themselves, where ideas can be challenged in a healthy way, people can take risks, and all of the key factors needed to create strong teams and organizations are present. In terms of creating synergy, effective communication helps keep the team at a high-performing phase.

What are some of those key factors?

■ Trust
Because the leader is listening to others, others listen to the leader. People actually start to voluntarily give feedback, because they see that their input is used to make changes. The bond of trust grows stronger, resulting in people feeling safe, supported, and open to more possibilities.

■ Ownership and Responsibility
When the channels of communication are open, people feel a part of the process. They feel more engaged in their work, take more responsibility, and are happy to be accountable for it.

■ Performance Standards Are Raised
When there is open communication, people feel valued, like their ideas and experiences count, resulting in an increased sense of pride in what they do. People expect more of themselves and give more. Ultimately, people want to feel that they matter.

MARK: *For over five years, I was the chair of a board that had major communication issues with the CEO. Instead of allowing information to flow, she tended to guard all of the portfolios to ensure that we were only hearing what she wanted us to hear. Information was only given one way. If anyone asked hard questions, she would start screaming that she wasn't being trusted, and would fly off the handle, sometimes even swearing at the board member who raised a concern. Needless to say, this created an incredibly toxic environment. One by one, I watched as my fellow board members closed down and gave up trying to communicate and understand what was going on with the organization. Many simply resigned because they refused to be treated like this.*

In the daily operations of the organization, things were no different. If directors tried something new, they were humiliated in front of the management team. There was no room for ideas to flow; anyone wanting to suggest anything innovative or wanting to take a risk was essentially told to shut up, to listen to what the boss had to say, or leave. This was an option a remarkable number of people decided to take. People became afraid of the reaction they would get from the leader if they did anything on their own. One by one, many of the directors stopped investing themselves in their departments; people became unmotivated and stopped caring about the outcome. In the course of five years, we lost six board members and five key management directors, and the project failed to reach its ultimate objectives. There were many factors, but the communication style of the leader certainly played an important part of the disappointing result.

LEADERS

■ TRAIT 5 REVIEW: Communicate Effectively

BEING A GREAT LEADER MEANS:
1. Paying Attention to the Words You Use
2. Noticing the Response You Get
3. Keeping Communication Flowing

KEY CONCEPT
By creating an open environment where ideas can be exchanged freely, people are clear and engaged in the process.

REALITY CHECK!
Often as a leader, we are afraid to allow people to say what they think, or to have two-way communication in case we hear what we don't want to know. To avoid this, leaders sometimes dictate or close themselves off from giving and getting constructive criticism. Effectively communicating means creating the kind of environment where people aren't afraid to express themselves. It enables ideas to flow and breakthroughs to happen.

Bring This Trait to Life
As different situations unfold, check in with yourself:
1. Are you creating a trusting environment where high-level communication happens?
2. Do people feel like their ideas are valued based on dialogue, debate, and feedback?
3. Do you take into consideration the feedback you are given as a leader, and apply it to make things better?

LEADERS

TRAIT 6:
Exemplify Excellence

KEY CONCEPT

By inspiring with your actions, you create a platform upon which others want to uphold their own standard of excellence.

MARK: *A top executive at one of the companies I worked with regularly brought his dog to work. Cute thing, everyone loved him, this dog was like the company mascot.*

Soon, though, several people started bringing their dogs to work as well. As you walked into the main reception area, you would be greeted by a number of dogs, all jumping up on you. It was getting out of hand, so a memo went around telling everyone that dogs were no longer allowed in the workplace. This was no problem for the employees—until they realized that the rule didn't apply to the top executive. He continued to bring his dog. Somehow, he was above the memo.

People were very annoyed and became quite cynical. In that single action of not following his own rules, this leader had lost all the credibility and trust of those he was leading. As drastic as it may sound, this incident was the beginning of the end for him.

Another leader potentially faced a similar fate, but managed to turn it around. He was a smoker, and as he started to stay at the office after regular business hours, he started to break the rules and not go outside, but instead smoked in his office. At first, it went unnoticed, but soon some of the other people working late who were also smokers came to his office to join him. By the second week, he was being interrupted every 40 minutes so that people could come by and smoke. He recognized that he had created the problem in the first place, and decided he needed to take drastic action to change things. He quit smoking. When people came to his office, the no smoking news was broken. The problem was solved. People still worked hard, and sometimes late, but the constant stopping for smoking breaks ended.

BEING A GREAT LEADER MEANS:
1. Taking a Hard Look in the Mirror
2. Being an Excellent Example
3. Holding Others Up as Examples

1. Taking a Hard Look in the Mirror

For most of the Leader Traits, the focus has been on connecting others to their best. Here, we turn the tables, asking you to look at yourself and reflect on the kind of example you are giving. This might not necessarily be fun, but answer the following questions as honestly as you can:

- Am I trustworthy?
- Am I supportive of others?
- Do I treat others with respect?
- Do I listen well?
- Is my energy consistently positive?
- Are my actions in line with my words?
- Do I recognize others' achievements?
- Am I approachable?

Take a minute to think about these basic leadership qualities.

Okay, now let's go through them again, this time taking the next step and asking yourself, "How did I last role-model each of these characteristics?" You might have answered yes to many of them, but do you actually display these characteristics to the people you are leading day in and day out? And what does it look like when you bring them to life?

- *How* do I show trustworthiness?
- *How* am I supportive of others?
- *How* do I treat others with respect?
- *How* do I listen well?
- *How* is my energy consistently positive?
- *How* are my actions in line with my words?
- *How* do I recognize other's achievements?
- *How* am I approachable?

Which of the above behaviors might you need to consciously make a point of doing better?

MARK: *If we don't hold up a mirror to ourselves, inevitably someone else will do it for us. When working with the International Olympic Committee, our mandate was to choose the best city possible for the best athletes of the world to have the best competition. But we got sidetracked taking gifts, letting our self-interest influence the process, and wining and dining with the bigwigs instead of truly doing our job properly. It was in the last city where we got busted.*

Nelson Mandela watched us getting organized for a photo with him after his presentation. We left the middle space for him, in between the oldest and most important members of the commission. When they called him to come in for the picture, Mr. Mandela went straight to the back, taking the youngest and least important person on the commission to the middle place in the front that had been reserved for him, and then returned to take her spot in the back for the picture. "Ready for the photo," he said. Without saying a word, he showed us not only that we were all equal here, but also how out of synch we were with our own purpose.

2. Being an Excellent Example

Role-modeling sets the tone for your environment. How you act and behave will be a visual guide for those you lead. It will ripple out and determine how those you are leading, in turn, will act and behave. Great leaders gain trust and respect from those they are leading by role modeling how they want them to be. This is why it is so important to start by being the example if you want others to be a specific way. A picture is worth a thousand words.

As a leader, part of your responsibility is to create the environment that enables others to excel. Role-modeling—how you act—affects others at the subconscious level. Consider this: Is there congruency between your words and actions? If someone were to walk into your environment, what would they notice or feel about it? Would they leave thinking to themselves that they would love to work there? Or would they be running for the hills? What tone are you setting by the way you are being?

DEBBIE: A number of years ago, I was coaching a large group of swimmers and got very angry because no one was listening to me. Everyone was talking among themselves, interrupting and arguing. I became so frustrated that I just walked out on them. I knew the moment I did it that it was absolutely the worst thing I could do.

Would it be acceptable for them to walk out of a practice if they became frustrated?

My thinking behind doing what I did was well intentioned. I wanted to do something drastic that would get them to start paying attention to me. The unintended result was that I got defiance and anger—not a good thing to have when you want world-class performance.

Beyond just setting a bad example, what does an action like that say at the subconscious level? Without even realizing it, these are some of the unintended messages I had sent out:

- She is giving up on us. *(I created doubts in the people I was leading.)*
- She doesn't think we're good enough. *(They lost belief in themselves.)*
- She solves problems by getting mad and then leaving. *(I don't go the distance.)*

- We'll never know when our leader will fly off the handle. *(I lost their trust.)*
- If the leader can storm out of here, so can I. *(It is okay to give up.)*

Great role-modeling has the power to build trust, gain credibility, earn respect, and create a productive environment. But it can have the opposite effect if we are not careful. A leader must remember that we are onstage every day. People are watching everything we do, the way we see things, how we behave. It all starts with your example. Great leaders inspire others to want to give their best because they don't want to let them down. That is being an excellent example.

3. Holding Others Up as Examples

Often people we lead show us examples of excellence day in and day out, especially when we have the right people doing the right roles. By pointing out these people's qualities, we give others an example to follow. In turn, this inspires others to greater performances and, at the same time, shows that you notice what they are doing well. That inspires more great action, and so on.

But there is something to be particularly aware of here. Human nature can sometimes get jealous and insecure around others' excellence. People can mistakenly think that if someone else is great, that might mean that they can't be. They compare themselves to others and get stuck in thinking it is an either/or situation.

Our job is to show them that there is enough room in this world for all of us to excel. But wait a minute! In sport, only one person wins the gold medal, right? On one hand, that is true, and at the same time, every day of training, every step of the way, there were people on the team that did their part. By everyone doing her or his own part excellently, that made everyone more excellent. When you are all working for the same company, that gold medal is the collective result, not one person's. Everyone doing their job to the best of their ability leads to winning results.

As a leader, when you regularly hold up others, be sure that everyone is clear that another's good example doesn't mean that they aren't

LEADERS

also great at what they do. People will come to understand that there are no limits on human capacity for excellence. When people really get this concept, instead of being jealous, they can be inspired by the greatness of each other.

MARK: *When I first started taking public speaking classes, the leader of our group did a perfect job at setting the stage for each of us to recognize that there was enough room for all of us in the class to be excellent.*

Each week, there was a small prize for the person who best exemplified a particular attribute in their presentations. You might expect that the class of forty adults, largely from sales backgrounds, would be competitive with each other, but the exact opposite reaction happened. We saw as each week went by that every one of us was good at something, and had valuable information to share with the group. Instead of fighting each other for the prizes, we encouraged each other. In the last weeks of the class, the shyest person had a breakthrough and wowed the entire room. She received a thunderous standing ovation from her peers. I have never forgotten that simple lesson that each of us is good at something, and if we can find a way to delight in the excellence of others, then at the same time we enable ourselves to delight in our own excellence.

■ TRAIT 6 REVIEW: Exemplify Excellence

BEING A GREAT LEADER MEANS:

1 Taking a Hard Look in the Mirror
2. Being an Excellent Example
3. Holding Others Up as Examples

KEY CONCEPT

By inspiring with your actions, you create a platform upon which others want to uphold their own standard of excellence.

REALITY CHECK!

Human nature is to get envious and a bit jealous when people around us are doing well. At first we celebrate with them, but if someone gets too much success, we somehow feel that says something bad about us. So, we start looking at them differently, focusing on their faults, and secretly enjoying their mishaps. Great leaders know how to avoid this pitfall. By being an excellent example and celebrating the many good things in different people around them, leaders remind people that we are all pretty great in our own way, and someone else's success can reflect our own capacity for excellence.

Bring This Trait to Life

As different situations unfold, check in with yourself:

1. When you hold the mirror up to yourself, is there congruence between what you say and what you do?
2. Do you celebrate excellence in others?
3. Does the environment you are creating by your example inspire champion results?

LEADERS

TRAIT 7:
Embrace Contradictions

KEY CONCEPT
By looking at multiple solutions to any given situation, you find what works even if that appears to contradict what you have done before.

MARK: *I have been involved in the Olympic movement for a long time. I was an athlete for sixteen years, and had gone on to become an executive board member of Toronto's Olympic bid, part of the athletes' commission for the International Aquatic Federation, as well as being a member of the Canadian Olympic Committee. Although I was still deeply committed to making a difference within the international sport scene, there came a moment when I seemed to completely contradict myself by stepping down from all of my involvements. How was leaving going to matter? Wasn't the best way to contribute to stay within?*

Under most circumstances, this might have held true. But following the Salt Lake City scandal, when deep-seated corruption within the Olympic movement made headlines around the world, there was an opportunity to face the serious problems and make a change for the better. Unfortunately, the leadership at that time was unwilling to take any personal responsibility or honestly face the situation. Looking at all of the solutions available at that time, leaving seemed to be the best option for me to actually take some meaningful actions.

Starting with a couple of athletes and corporate supporters from Canada, and growing quickly to become an international grassroots campaign of advocates and athletes from around the world, we created Olympic Athletes Together Honorably (OATH), an organization that put pressure to reform from the outside. We were accused by many of trying to destroy the Olympic movement, but that wasn't our intention at all. As legendary swimmer John Naber put it, "We don't want to take over the running of international sport. We don't want a piece of the pie. We just want to make sure the pie tastes as good as the recipe intended it to." Even though we appeared to be contradicting ourselves by speaking against the Olympic leaders, our actions were driven from a place of values, namely how much we cared about preserving all that was good within the movement.

In the end, our group created a 93-page comprehensive report giving an overview of what was necessary to move toward an ethical foundation for Olympic reform. Interestingly, there were many people on the inside who were change-minded, and this report gave them the leverage to push some of the reform agenda forward. It was the combination of the people on the inside and what was being done on the outside that in the end helped shape the reform process.

BEING A GREAT LEADER MEANS:
1. Accepting the Nature of Paradox
2. Mastering the Art and Science of Leadership
3. Respecting Core Values and Providing Rationale

1. Accepting the Nature of Paradox

Extreme ideas, seemingly in opposition, can sometimes work brilliantly together. The following groupings are just a few examples of contradictions that we face putting ideas into action. Among them, there is no wrong or right statement, just notions from opposite ends of the spectrum to be used in different circumstances.

Take a risk.
Be cautious.

Plan meticulously.
Go with the flow.

Be patient.
Go now!

Be consistent.
Change it up.

Use logic.
Follow your gut.

Work hard.
Have fun.

Don't compromise.
Be flexible.

The secret is to find the way that works most effectively in any given situation. Leadership means taking the idea of doing what works, as

LEADERS

opposed to what was right or wrong, to the next level by embracing contradictions. We understand that there is no absolute right or wrong because there is never just one way to get something done. There may be one outcome we are striving for, but there are always several different possibilities to take us there. It is up to us to decide what is the best in any given situation. Different things work for different people—we are not all the same. A great leader is able to adapt what we do to meet the needs of each individual.

Sometimes that will mean intervening.
Other times we will stand back.

Sometimes it will mean giving feedback immediately.
Other times we will wait.

Sometimes we will give control.
At other times, we will take it.

Sometimes we will listen.
Other times we will talk.

The point here is that there is no wrong or right. It is doing what works best for the people we are leading, even if that appears to contradict what we have done before.

2. Mastering the Art and Science of Leadership

We believe that you can read every book on leadership, develop every skill set, understand rationally all the steps necessary to become a leader, and still not have all that it takes. That is because leadership is also about ambiguities, perceptions, and feelings. Take communication as an example. It is the combination of knowing the right words to use (a skill) with the right timing (a feeling) that makes for great communication.

Leadership encompasses two seemingly contradictory concepts. On one hand, we have the practical, rational, pragmatic, step-by-step approach that we call the science of leadership. On the other hand, we have the concept that is harder to quantify. It is the sense of things, the gut feeling, the instinct that something is working or not, that we call the art of leadership. It is the marriage of these two seemingly contradictory elements that creates great leaders.

What this means in terms of embracing contradictions is that great leaders know not just what to do, but also when to do it, and know not just for themselves, but for others, too.

DEBBIE: I have had the opportunity to observe an up-and-coming coach as part of my mentoring responsibilities. Watching him in different situations, I noticed that he tended to go to yelling as his primary way of communicating with his athletes when he got frustrated. After observing a training session, I asked him what he was trying to get across, and showed him that yelling might not be the best way to do it. He agreed, and worked on alternative, more effective ways of giving feedback to his athletes, especially in the heat of the moment of competition.

Many months later, I was there when once again he was yelling at his team. Although I would typically never condone this kind of behavior, in this particular instance it was the exact right thing to do. His athletes needed a jolt, and the best way to do that was to yell at them. I sat with the coach after, and told him I liked the way he had handled the situation. "But I thought you didn't like it when I yell?" he asked. And usually I didn't. But that is the nuance of leadership, knowing what to do when, and determining what is the right thing to do in any particular moment, even if it seems to contradict what we have said and done before.

3. Respecting Core Values and Providing Rationale

You may be willing to do whatever works, but the one thing that should never get compromised or contradicted are your values. Let them guide the process. As a leader, we must also be able to clearly identify the rationale behind making the choices we do. When embracing contradiction, it is very important to be clear on why we are doing what we are doing, and how that relates back to the larger objective.

It can be confusing if you are doing one thing one day, and then take an entirely different approach the next. It can open the door for distrust because people might not know how to read you. You have to be careful. If someone asks why you are doing something that seems like a contradiction and they hear you respond, "Because I say so," chances are they won't buy in. But if you can be clear on why you are dong what you are doing, then people will tend to support you. They will see that no matter what you do, you will be coming from a place of looking for what will work best.

MARK: *I was part of a company whose leader had an unfortunate habit of saying one thing one day, and then doing a complete 180-degree turn the next. People never knew what to expect. You'd come in on Monday and be his best friend, come in Tuesday and he wouldn't even acknowledge you were there. He'd tell the team one day to focus on growing the business in Europe. Three days later, he would be angry because the team wasn't working on the American market. He continually contradicted himself.*

Slowly, the directors lost all of their confidence in him. They didn't want to bother investing in what he asked of them because they knew they would be asked to do something completely different as soon as they started down one path. The problem was that their leader was constantly in reactionary mode, not acting from a place of purpose that people could rally behind, but basing his strategy on a whim. He constantly contradicted himself without any rationale, and wasn't making the best decisions for the team. Eventually, the respect and solidarity of his people evaporated. His results fell well short of the intended outcome, mostly because he was surrounded in the end by yes people and not the best people.

■ TRAIT 7 REVIEW: Embrace Contradictions

BEING A GREAT LEADER MEANS:
1. Accepting the Nature of Paradox
2. Mastering the Art and Science of Leadership
3. Respecting Core Values and Providing Rationale

KEY CONCEPT
By looking at multiple solutions to any given situation, you find what works even if that appears to contradict what you have done before.

REALITY CHECK!
Often as leaders, we are fearful of being seen as contradictory. We don't want to be known for constantly changing our minds, or going a different route on a whim. In order to counteract this, we become more strict and rigid in our approach. We don't want to appear like we are losing control. Embracing contradictions means staying open to what works best in any given situation and letting go of that fear. It enables us to make the best decisions possible, and the freedom to be great.

Bring This Trait to Life
As different situations unfold, check in with yourself:
1. Are you looking at several alternative solutions in different situations?
2. Do you make decisions based on what works instead of what is right or wrong?
3. Are your decisions consistent with your values?

LEADERS

TRAIT 8:
Continually Evolve

KEY CONCEPT
By creating a dynamic environment where the bar is constantly being raised, excellence is fostered and winning results happen.

DEBBIE: Our story ends back where it started. Mark and I began our personal and professional journey together when he had gotten complacent and stopped evolving. Ranked second in the world, he made the mistake that so many of us do. He had thought he had it all figured out, and that if he simply kept doing what he was doing, then he would remain on top of his game. That way of thinking caught up with him, and forced him to change in order to get to the next level, which, in his case, was to become a champion and win the Olympics.

In a sense, that was where this book was first born. For twenty years, I had refined my own approach as a coach who could lead synchronized swimmers to excellence, and working with Mark helped me further evolve by applying those ideas to a completely new and different environment. That first year Mark and I worked together, we would spend countless hours exploring the ideas that would one day become this book.

Over ten years ago, we had started to write a book together, but at that particular juncture, the timing wasn't right for us. The ideas were all there, but we needed more time to evolve, to apply these concepts in different ways with others to further clarify for ourselves what the fundamentals were. I went on to work with businesses, and eventually came back to the sport system, leading a team that reviewed all of the summer and winter sports to connect them to higher levels of performance. Mark went on to work within the political side of international sport, and then to television, speaking and leading social change movements. Even though we weren't officially writing or working together, further exploring the ideas we had started as coach and athlete became the basis of our long-standing friendship.

This book has been a testament to the idea of continually evolving. When we came back together to make another attempt at writing, the timing was absolutely right. But the book changed forms dozens of times from when we began to the product you are holding in your hands now. The fundamental ideas never changed, but how we expressed them went through constant refinement. We started with baby steps, and once one trait came together, it gave us the confidence to move to the next. Over the course of many, many months, we gained the momentum needed to finally turn those independent ideas into a book. Looking back to the experience that brought us together close to twenty years ago, we had to apply that same thinking to evolve to where we are today.

Continually
Evolve

■ TRAIT 8

BEING A GREAT LEADER MEANS:
1. Building Momentum
2. Having High Expectations
3. Encouraging a Culture of Improvement

1. Building Momentum

Many of us have seen that success breeds further success. The small wins we have with those we are leading fuels their belief in themselves and what they are a part of, which then makes it possible to achieve better and better results. What you do today impacts what you are able to do tomorrow. When you have a small success, the bar can be raised a bit higher for the next day, and then the next, and the next, and so on. Success builds on itself, creating momentum that keeps raising the bar and moving everyone forward and upward. But it all has to start somewhere.

There are a couple of misperceptions about achieving great results. The first is that in order to achieve fantastic outcomes, huge things have to happen. In reality, it is the small steps that eventually make the big difference. Over time, it is the accumulation of these little successes that lead to world-class performances and champion results. The second misperception is that every day has to be better than the last. It doesn't work like that. Continually evolving is also about persevering through the hard times and facing setbacks. The difference is that a great leader has the ability to find some small success even if the day is a disaster. Learning from what is not working to find what will work is what keeps momentum building.

MARK: *A colleague of mine was a junior account manager for an ad agency. For a long time, she was very excited about work and the challenges it presented, but eventually she found herself getting bored and restless as her work became routine. Her job was no longer stimulating and she started to develop a bad attitude, losing the momentum that had once made her great.*

Luckily, she had a wise boss who understood that he needed to provide her with greater challenges or risk losing her. He took a chance and put her in as the lead of a huge account for a new client, raising the bar for her and creating a new momentum. She faced some tough times

LEADERS

along the way, but rising to this challenge stimulated her again, and she turned her deteriorating interest and success around. Her boss had taken a calculated risk, but he believed in her ability to do the job and knew she had to grow and be challenged. This helped her evolve to a new level. The risk turned out to be a good one. The campaign that she created for the client went on to win numerous national and international awards.

2. Having High Expectations

People tend to live up to what they believe your expectations are of them. If you expect too little from people, that is likely what you will get. Never underestimate the capacity of the people you work with to be great.

But how do you continually set the bar higher without overwhelming people, or making them feel like no matter what they do, it is never good enough? This is where the art of leadership comes in, using your heightened awareness to increase expectations in such a way that is empowering and motivating to those you are leading. It is finding those coachable moments when you know someone is in a place where they are ready to be challenged, and they can take what you have to say. Timing is critical in knowing when to raise the bar, and by how much. Done poorly, people feel that you, as a leader, are never satisfied, which translates into an unmotivated person who limits his or her own potential. Done well, raising the bar helps people evolve.

Great leaders constantly have high expectations for others. As you raise expectations, it is crucial to make sure that you are providing the training and tools necessary to achieve the higher expectations. We can't expect performance and results to get better if we haven't provided the resources necessary to get people to the next level. Appropriate training and resources go hand in hand with higher expectations.

DEBBIE: I recall training for the World Aquatic Championships at the University of Toronto pool. One day, our consultant from Sport Canada came to have a meeting with me. Unfortunately, the day he chose to observe, we were having a lot of trouble with our execution. It was the end of a high-volume training period and everyone was tired. Following the workout, I met with the consultant.

"What are your performance goals for the World Championships?" he asked.

"Three gold medals," was my reply.

There was a long pause, and then he countered, "Are you sure you want to commit to that? It's a bit of a long shot, don't you think?"

"I know it's a big stretch but we believe we can achieve it," I said.

"Okay, but you don't have to say that. If you tell me you want three gold medals and we put it down on paper and you don't achieve it, that's going to look like you failed," he said.

"And we will have failed," I replied. "I believe we can win three and I don't want to lower that expectation."

"Well, judging from what I saw today, you'll be lucky if you win one," he said.

I countered, "The goal is three gold medals and we're not settling for anything less. We've raised the bar and are committed to it. I don't want to play it safe."

A month later, we won all three events at the World Aquatic Championships. There were some nail-biting moments for sure, but I don't think it would have happened if we hadn't clearly stated that that was our goal and we were willing to take it public. Our expectations were high, the training program that could get the athletes to a level that matched our expectations was provided, and the results followed suit.

3. Encouraging a Culture of Improvement

It is human nature to resist change, but whether we like it or not, the world around us is constantly evolving. What is accepted as a great result today might not be so good tomorrow. That is why it is important to keep your expectations high. So, how do we challenge ourselves from getting complacent?

A large part of that is creating an environment that values evolution, where people feel safe to take risks and make mistakes. Often, the way we evolve is through trial and error. If we expect perfection every time, then there is no room to explore. People get paralyzed with fear,

LEADERS

stuck doing what might have worked at one time, but not being able to adapt and evolve to find what is needed to work now. By allowing people to take risks and make mistakes, you create an environment where people can tap into their potential. Keep in mind that mistakes are acceptable, but making the same mistake time and again is not.

This is not to say that people don't get bogged down periodically anyway. They do. But there are ways to help them get past this. Identify their strengths, determine how they can best use them, and help them with a plan that will lead to an area where they can apply their talents and begin to tap into their full potential again. Some elements are constants, like core values and a fixed purpose. The leader's job is to stimulate improvement in everything else. Creating the environment where this can happen requires another constant—evaluation. That starts by making sure that *you* as a leader are constantly evaluating your own performance and evolving. This brings us right back to where this whole journey started—the first Achiever Trait, where we saw that by mastering the question, you connect to yourself *and* to what you want to achieve.

1. What do I need to learn?
2. How can I capitalize on others' knowledge to improve?
3. How can I raise the bar for myself and those I am leading?

■ TRAIT 8 REVIEW: Continually Evolve

BEING A GREAT LEADER MEANS:
1. Building Momentum
2. Having High Expectations
3. Encouraging a Culture of Improvement

KEY CONCEPT
By creating a dynamic environment where the bar is constantly being raised, excellence is fostered and winning results happen.

REALITY CHECK!
There is a really fine line between continuing to do what you've done because it is working, and knowing when to evolve to do things in a different and better way. You do not want to constantly change things that are working, and at the same time you do not want to wait until they don't work. By creating an environment where people can make mistakes—and they will—change will always be welcome. Continually evolving creates a culture that is always challenging itself to become better.

Bring This Trait to Life
As different situations unfold, check in with yourself:
1. Are you building on small successes with those you are leading?
2. Is the bar being raised with expectations getting set higher?
3. Do people feel supported to take risks in a dynamic environment?

LEADERS

KEY CONCEPT SYNOPSIS
THE LEADER TRAITS
Creating Champion Organizations and Teams

 The greater your awareness, the greater your capacity to act effectively as a leader.

 By creating an open environment where ideas can be exchanged freely, people are clear and are engaged in the process.

 By capturing people's imagination with a clear objective, you inspire every individual to do their part in making it happen.

 By inspiring with your actions, you create a platform upon which others want to uphold their own standard of excellence.

 By bringing together the right people, an inexplicable energy is created that produces winning results much greater than any one individual's contribution.

 By looking at multiple solutions to any given situation, you can find what works even if that appears to contradict what you have done before.

 By being passionate and believing completely in what you are doing, it enables you and the people you lead to break through enormous obstacles.

 By creating a dynamic environment where the bar is constantly being raised, excellence is fostered and winning results happen.

LEADER TRAITS—SELF ASSESSMENT

Before moving on in this book, take the time to complete this quick, simple evaluation tool. See what Leader Traits need more work than others and invest some time in them.

Rate yourself on a scale of 1 to 4:
1 = Strongly Disagree, 2 = Disagree, 3 = Agree, 4 = Strongly Agree

Leader Trait	Personal Life	Professional Life
1. Be Aware I consciously think about how I can frame my thoughts to be more empowering for myself and those I lead.	1 2 3 4	1 2 3 4
Actions to Improve		
I help those I am leading be aware of their empowering and limiting thoughts, and how they can use them to create winning results.	1 2 3 4	1 2 3 4
Actions to Improve		
2. Have Purpose Everyone on the team clearly knows what the objective/ winning result is.	1 2 3 4	1 2 3 4
Actions to Improve		
I have a clear plan, including the role and targets for each person involved.	1 2 3 4	1 2 3 4
Actions to Improve		

LEADERS

Leader Trait		Personal Life	Professional Life
3. Create Synergy I have the right people in the right roles.		1 2 3 4	1 2 3 4
Actions to Improve			
The team is performing at the Phase 4: High Performance level.		1 2 3 4	1 2 3 4
Actions to Improve			
4. Show Conviction I believe completely in what we are doing and the objectives we have established.		1 2 3 4	1 2 3 4
Actions to Improve			
I am able to lead everyone through the tough times and instil confidence in what we are doing.		1 2 3 4	1 2 3 4
Actions to Improve			

LEADERS

Leader Trait	Personal Life	Professional Life
5. Communicate Effectively My words and actions communicate the points I want to get across.	1 2 3 4	1 2 3 4
Actions to Improve		
I have created an open environment where ideas and feedback are freely exchanged.	1 2 3 4	1 2 3 4
Actions to Improve		
6. Exemplify Excellence The example I set is the one I want others to follow.	1 2 3 4	1 2 3 4
Actions to Improve		
I often hold up others as examples of excellence.	1 2 3 4	1 2 3 4
Actions to Improve		

LEADERS

Leader Trait		Personal Life	Professional Life
7. Embrace Contradictions I look for "what will work" in any given situation, as opposed to what I have always done before.		1 2 3 4	1 2 3 4
Actions to Improve			
I am able to provide rationale for all decisions and actions that I make.			
Actions to Improve			
8. Continually Evolve I continuously raise the bar to create a high performing environment for all.		1 2 3 4	1 2 3 4
Actions to Improve			
I maximize small successes to create positive momentum.			
Actions to Improve			

The Legacy Traits
*Championing a
Meaningful Way of Life*

Each of the Legacy Traits has a graphic icon highlighted in orange to help support the key ideas found within.

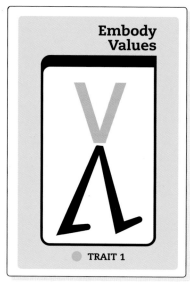

Embody Values

TRAIT 1

TRAIT 1:
The V on the stick legs reminds us to bring our values to life.

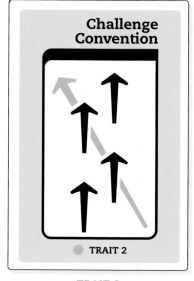

Challenge Convention

TRAIT 2

TRAIT 2:
The one arrow crossing the others represents the importance to sometimes go against popular thinking.

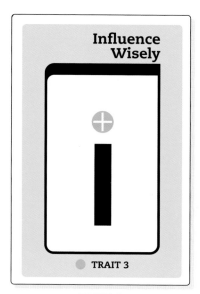

Influence Wisely

TRAIT 3

TRAIT 3:
The plus sign (+) reminds us of the opportunity we all have to make a positive impact on others.

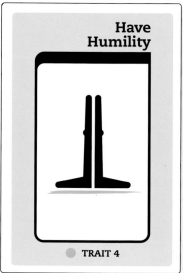

Have Humility

TRAIT 4

TRAIT 4:
The knobby-kneed figure reminds us to stay humble and grounded.

LEGACY

Use all eight icons as visual reminders of the key concepts and ideas within each of the Legacy Traits.

Show Goodwill

TRAIT 5

TRAIT 5:
The smiling face in motion represents the kindness with which we can move through life.

Celebrate Humanity

TRAIT 6

TRAIT 6:
The globe simply represents the larger world we are all a part of.

Live Now

TRAIT 7

TRAIT 7:
The alarm clock reminds us to wake up this moment.

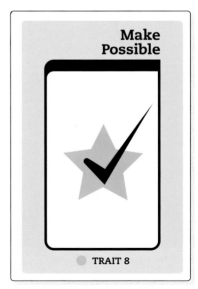

Make Possible

TRAIT 8

TRAIT 8:
The check in the star represents that you can make things happen for yourself and others.

LEGACY

N The Legacy Traits, we take the final step on *The Champion's Journey*. What do we mean when we speak of legacy? For us, ultimately this is about creating a lasting win by making a positive impact on the world. It is about considering the future, the possibility of betterment, the expansion of meaningful ideas and actions. Legacy happens by example, and has the possibility to positively impact thousands and thousands of people who we come into contact with. Little seemingly incidental actions taken by us can leave a lasting impression on others.

The irony with the Legacy Traits is that you can't really teach them. Legacy just is. There is no action plan, step-by-step approach to them. They just are. This part of the book reminds you of simple truths to champion a more meaningful way of being.

It is important to realize that you leave a legacy with your life. It doesn't matter which title you have, or how many—CEO, web designer, coach, corner store cashier, nurse, neighbor, parent, community activist, teacher, son, builder, mother-in-law, whatever. Simply as human beings, we are remembered for how we are. We celebrate all our *achievements*—individual and collective, personal and professional—largely because of the people that we encountered and connected with. The Legacy Traits ask you to consider the following:

1. How am I moving through the world?
2. Am I leaving this _____ (job, relationship, park) better than I found it?
3. What kind of impact will the actions I am taking have over the long term?

What you will find within each Legacy Trait is a key concept that comes to life with an example of a well-known person who exemplifies each of the eight traits. The point here is not that these people had huge success, but that we recognize, fame or not, all of us leave some kind of legacy, often based on who we are. Our actions ripple out far beyond what we could ever imagine. We hope the Legacy Traits inspire you to remember and recognize some of the people in your life who matter but can too easily be taken for granted in the daily rush. At the end of each of the eight traits is a Review with fundamental questions to help you keep the idea of legacy in mind. And at the very end of the Legacy section is an evaluation tool to guide you in identifying where you are already strong, and where you might have to make more of a conscious effort to improve.

Join us on this final step that rounds out *The Champion's Journey*.

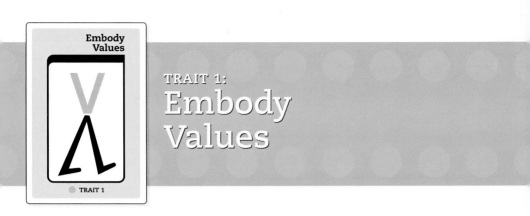

TRAIT 1:
Embody Values

KEY CONCEPT
Know yourself. Your values act as a compass, guiding your decision making, showing people who you are.

Your values give your life solid ground. When you understand what is important to you, champion those core ideals by bringing them to life. It gives you a sense of harmony and congruency. What you value will be unique, and how you live your values might change from situation to situation. But, at the end of the day, your actions and what you stand for can consistently be traced back to the values you believe in.

A Legendary Example of This Trait

Kim Phuc is one of the most famous subjects of a photograph the world has ever seen. Caught in war, she was the girl in the middle of the road, burned so severely she would need to stay in the hospital for 14 months, an unforgettable image of the Vietnam tragedy. Named a UNESCO Goodwill Ambassador twenty years later, she now values peace and forgiveness. Her personal bravery enabled her, on the way back to Cuba following her honeymoon, to get off the plane during a refueling stop in Canada and ask for political asylum. Today she is part of a strong community, has a husband and a family—and has found peace within to be able to speak out through the work she does. She was asked to give a speech at the U.S. Vietnam Veterans' Day Memorial in Washington, DC, on Veterans' Day, and briefly met a man who was part of the team that ordered the bomb to be dropped on her. She listened intensely to his story, and then she forgave him. Kim Phuc leaves a legacy everywhere she goes by embodying the values she believes in.

Who do you know that shows this trait?

DEBBIE: I work with a coach who places a high value on respecting others. For a special session with a guest instructor, eight of his athletes were two minutes late. He felt this was completely disrespectful and didn't let them attend the session. Embodying values can be hard, but it makes an impression. The next week they were all ten minutes early.

Take a moment to think about people in your life. Who lives this legacy trait? It might be family, friends, an everyday encounter, a person from the past. Who embodies values?

● TRAIT 1 REVIEW: Embody Values

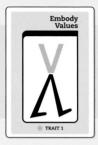

KEY CONCEPT

Know yourself. Your values act as a compass, guiding your decision making, showing people who you are.

REALITY CHECK!

Many of us aren't very clear about what we really value. It is hard to embody something you aren't aware of. When you are clear on what you stand for, you are able to stand for what you value.

Bring This Trait to Life

To make a difference, consider the following:

1. What values are important to you?
2. How do your values show up in your day-to-day living?
3. Are there better ways you can champion the values you believe in?

LEGACY

Challenge
Convention

TRAIT 2

TRAIT 2:
Challenge Convention

KEY CONCEPT

Break free from the status quo. Having the courage to challenge popular ideas often leads to breakthroughs and paves the way for others to follow.

Collective group thinking doesn't make it right or even truthful—it simply makes it popular. Conventional wisdom is conventional for a reason: The majority of the people think it. This doesn't mean that tradition isn't valuable. It can be. But if you never challenged what came before you, you would never have found the breakthroughs that brought you to where you are today, and that will take you further in the future.

A Legendary Example of this Trait

Roger Bannister became a track and field legend. While at Oxford, he drew attention from the media and school officials. He chose to forego the 1948 Olympics for his medical studies, and then in 1952, although British champion, came fourth at the Olympics in his best event. The media scorned him, so he set out to prove them wrong. To redeem himself, he decided to break the world record for the mile, and be the first person under the four-minute barrier. Although still a full-time medical student with only 45 minutes a day to train, he thought he could do it despite what others thought. On May 6, 1954, at Oxford University, a 25-year-old Roger Bannister made history by running the mile in 3 minutes 59.4 seconds. Within a month, someone else had broken the record. But Roger Bannister broke it first, and by doing so, enabled many others to see themselves doing it, too.

Who do you know that shows this trait?

MARK: *We have a friend who is the queen of retail, and who does it on her own terms. In an era where stores are open 24/7, even though she is situated in the middle of one of Calgary's more unique shopping districts, she is closed on Mondays and Tuesdays, and is only open from noon to 5 p.m. on the other days. And, in spite of her unconventional hours, she is hugely successful!*

Take a moment to think about people in your life. Who lives this legacy trait? It might be family, friends, an everyday encounter, a person from the past. Who challenges convention?

LEGACY

● TRAIT 2 REVIEW: Challenge Convention

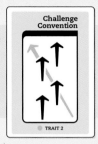

KEY CONCEPT

Break free from the status quo. Having the courage to challenge popular ideas often leads to breakthroughs and paves the way for others to follow.

REALITY CHECK!

Often, we are afraid to go against the grain because of what we fear the consequences might be. We could get hurt, look foolish, or get in trouble. Challenging convention enables us to find ways of doing things differently, and usually inspires others at the same time.

Bring This Trait to Life

To make a difference, consider the following:

1. When have you gotten stuck blindly accepting the status quo?
2. Can you champion a better way of doing things?
3. What different actions can you take that challenge you to be better?

LEGACY

TRAIT 3:
Influence Wisely

KEY CONCEPT

Recognize your impact. Generously share your wisdom, knowledge, and experience with others.

Whether it is peer to peer, one generation to the next, or one culture to another, we ALL have influence. But how do you use it? You can manipulate situations for your own benefit, always putting yourself first. Or you can encourage, praise, and share experiences selflessly with others so they don't have to make the same mistakes you did. Which way are you using your influence? Influencing wisely doesn't necessarily mean being touchy and feely, it might be tough love. The point is that you take a genuine interest in helping others move forward.

A Legendary Example of this Trait

Anita Roddick was best known for founding The Body Shop. She was trained as a teacher, married and opened a restaurant and a hotel, and worked for the United Nations where she traveled extensively and met people from many different cultures. The Body Shop, founded in 1976, always had an edge of social responsibility. Products were not tested on

157

animals, and recycling made practical sense. Those simple ideas led to over 77 million customers a year. She cared deeply about people, especially disenfranchised and forgotten children. She founded Children of the Edge as a response to the Eastern Europe orphan crisis. She had been one of those caught in pre-screening blood tragedies, contracting Hepatitis C, and revealed this publicly in order to raise awareness for others. Anita Roddick used her life to make a difference on every front for other people.

Who do you know that shows this trait?

MARK: *When my dad was receiving chemotherapy, a nurse approached me. She told me she was sorry that my family was going through this hard experience. She gently squeezed my arm, looked me in the eyes, and said, "Spend as much time as you can with him." Thanks to the way she handled the situation, I understood I had limited time to be with my dad. Her words influenced me to be there for the few remaining weeks before he died.*

Take a moment to think about people in your life. Who lives this legacy trait? It might be family, friends, an everyday encounter, a person from the past. Who influences wisely?

LEGACY

● TRAIT 3 REVIEW: Influence Wisely

KEY CONCEPT
Recognize your impact. Generously share your wisdom, knowledge, and experience with others.

REALITY CHECK!
We often underestimate our own experience and the wisdom we have gained, and don't even think to share it. Who do I think I am to speak up? To share something? But often we don't say what is obvious to us because we assume others know it. By wisely sharing our experience and perspective, we positively influence those around us.

Bring This Trait to Life
To make a difference, consider the following:
1. What are some situations where you can positively influence others?
2. What unique experience can you share with others to help move them forward?
3. How are people around you influencing you?

LEGACY

Have
Humility

TRAIT 4

TRAIT 4:
Have Humility

KEY CONCEPT
Check your ego. Acknowledge contributions, admit mistakes freely, and shine the light on others.

Keep your own sense of self-importance in perspective. Moving from a "me" centered to a "we" focus requires confidence. But there is a great ripple effect in being able to help others shine without needing all of the credit. Stand back and simply marvel at being a part of something great. Having humility doesn't mean not being proud; it just means taking a more humble approach that comes from the security of knowing the role you played without needing all of the fanfare.

A Legendary Example of this Trait

John Wooden is widely regarded as the greatest college coach in history—although he would never say that. His athletes won 665 games in 27 seasons, and ten NCAA titles during his last 12 tries, 7 of them consecutively. "A player who makes a team great is more valuable than a great player. Losing yourself in the group, for the good of the group, that is teamwork." His simple philosophies have become legendary, his seven-point creed showing exactly who he is. Although he is regarded as one of the best of the very, very best there ever was in terms of team coaching, his mantras include helping others, giving thanks, and making friendship a fine art. For his ability to bring out the best in others without needing to take all of the credit, John Wooden has left a legacy of leadership with grace.

Who do you know that shows this trait?

DEBBIE: A colleague of mine was leading a major change within her organization. After informing someone that they were being let go, she received some new information. After thinking for many hours, she called back the person she had fired and admitted she might have acted too hastily and reversed her decision. She didn't let her pride stand in the way of doing the right thing.

Take a moment to think about people in your life. Who lives this legacy trait? It might be family, friends, an everyday encounter, a person from the past. Who has humility?

● TRAIT 4 REVIEW: Have Humility

KEY CONCEPT
Check your ego. Acknowledge contributions, admit mistakes freely, and shine the light on others.

REALITY CHECK!
Sometimes we can overestimate our own importance, forgetting about the reality that with us or not, life carries on. The biggest limiting factor is that our egos get in the way, and we can't deny that we all have one. We don't want to make a mistake, or step back and let others get credit, because we think this reflects badly on us. Which is why when we do actually step back and let other people shine, when we do admit a mistake easily, when we really have humility, we make a positive impression.

Bring This Trait to Life
To make a difference, consider the following:
1. Are there times when your feeling of self-importance might be limiting you?
2. How would acting differently affect the outcome?
3. Are you championing those who support you behind the scenes?

LEGACY

TRAIT 5:
Show Goodwill

KEY CONCEPT
Be kind. The way you respond, react, or simply are in situations can have an enormous impact on those around you.

The world is not a perfect place. As you encounter people, it is easy to criticize, to find faults, to draw attention to mistakes, and to put others down. It takes more of a conscious effort to give people the benefit of the doubt, to allow for a difference of opinion. Goodwill can be as simple as smiling, saying thank you, or being polite and courteous. It is about building bridges instead of tearing them down, extending a hand instead of walking away.

A Legendary Example of this Trait

Jimmy Carter was the thirty-ninth President of the United States, and is recognized today for his 25 years of writing, peacekeeping, and humanitarian efforts since he left office. He is involved in many national and international committees on public policy, conflict resolution, and human rights. He is a best-selling author and a Nobel Peace Prize winner. He and his wife, Rosalynn, are well known for their work as volunteers for Habitat for Humanity, a program that helps low-income working people build and purchase their own homes. Seen hammering away, smiling at the other volunteers, Jimmy Carter exudes the good-will that has humanized his legacy.

Who do you know that shows this trait?

MARK: *I was the master of ceremonies at an event that ran overtime and ended at 5:25 p.m., and I was catching a 5:50 p.m. train. We were all set to make the tight time line until we realized backing up that we had a flat tire. With thousands of people leaving, and no taxis in sight, and no transportation, I went to the first car I saw and asked if we could get a ride to the station. "Hop in," the stranger said. We loaded the car, enjoyed the short trip, and made the train by five minutes.*

Take a moment to think about people in your life. Who lives this legacy trait? It might be family, friends, an everyday encounter, a person from the past. Who shows goodwill?

● TRAIT 5 REVIEW: Show Goodwill

KEY CONCEPT
Be kind. The way you respond, react, or simply are in situations can have an enormous impact on those around you.

REALITY CHECK!
We get so ingrained in our own lives that we just don't take the time to see how easy it is to give someone a smile, or go a bit out of our way to do something nice for another person. We get too caught up in our checklist of activities to show goodwill. But when you do, what comes back in terms of feeling good about yourself, you just can't put a price tag on.

Bring This Trait to Life
To make a difference, consider the following:
1. Were you thoughtful and considerate today?
2. Did you notice how your actions touched people around you?
3. How does it make you feel when someone shows you good-will?

LEGACY

Celebrate Humanity

TRAIT 6

TRAIT 6:
Celebrate Humanity

KEY CONCEPT

Appreciate diversity. We share common ground as human beings, and at the same time, we are all different and unique.

We live in societies surrounded by people of different nationalities, cultures, gender, ages, sexuality, and means. While each and every one of us is unique, collectively we share some common ground. Celebrating humanity means finding ways to showcase and highlight the best of what each of us brings to life. When our diversity is truly respected and nurtured, then we have an opportunity to share who we are for the benefit of all.

A Legendary Example of this Trait

Bono is best known as the lead singer and principal lyricist of the Irish rock band, U2. But he is also recognized on the world stage as someone who is dedicated to making a difference for people. Beginning in 1979 at a benefit concert, his activism has led not only to songwriting motivated by political, social, and religious themes; he has taken significant action. Widely known for his work concerning Africa, he has been campaigning since 1999 for third world debt relief, meeting with political world leaders, and raising awareness for the injustices on the African continent. Well beyond the Grammys, Bono has made an impact championing the rights of other people, which has earned him an honorary Knighthood, TIME Person of the Year, and three nominations for the Nobel Peace Prize.

Who do you know that shows this trait?

MARK: *I worked with a man who knew what it was like to be ostracized: as a child, he had grown up with polio. We met through the Special Olympians, the intellectually challenged kids where the gold medalist is happy to swap for the silver because he likes the color. These athletes capture the true spirit of sport. Special Olympic participants couldn't afford programs and travel, so he did something about it. Asking his friends to ask their friends to ask their friends, he raised millions of dollars to ensure that these kids that are filled with greatness get to celebrate their humanity on the playing field.*

Take a moment to think about people in your life. Who lives this legacy trait? It might be family, friends, an everyday encounter, a person from the past. Who celebrates humanity?

● TRAIT 6 REVIEW: Celebrate Humanity

KEY CONCEPT

Appreciate diversity. We share common ground as human beings, and at the same time, we are all different and unique.

REALITY CHECK!

Human nature has two equal and opposite sides. One side is to celebrate humanity, the other is to attack difference. We believe that differences need to be recognized, supported, and celebrated. It is not about everybody trying to be the same. The tough part is that our own culture is ingrained in us, and it is hard to step outside of that and see the validity of other perspectives. The more we can do that, the richer and more dimensional our celebration of humanity makes us.

Bring This Trait to Life
To make a difference, consider the following:
1. What makes you and those around you unique?
2. How do you champion and celebrate those qualities?
3. Are you creating the space for others to share their cultures and experiences?

LEGACY

TRAIT 7:
Live Now

KEY CONCEPT

Embrace the moment. Whatever that looks like and however it feels, this moment is as it should be.

This moment is as it is—it is not good or bad, it simply is. And from it, anything can happen. It is so easy to wait for life. When things are better (like when we have more money, more time, more space, more something), then you think you will be able to make a difference. The truth is you have today. This is not to say that you don't think about the future. You do. But you don't wait for that future to come; you make it happen by living now. This is it. Find what makes you feel inspired, excited, and alive, and then act on it.

A Legendary Example of this Trait

Richard Branson is an entrepreneur best known for the hip Virgin brand all over the world. A man who has never waited for anything to happen, his empire began at 16 when he published his first magazine. By 21, he had already set up a mail-order business and a chain of record stores. The Virgin brand was born on the spot, when all of the young *partners were "virgins" in business. Every moment of his life seems to be spent doing something extraordinary beyond business—from chasing and breaking world records in ballooning and amphibious vehicles, funding The Elders (a collective of former world leaders who use their skills to catalyze peaceful resolutions), to investing an estimated $3 billion in research for environmentally friendly fuels. Richard Branson's ability to completely embrace life wherever he finds himself is where his leadership legacy lies.*

Who do you know that shows this trait?

DEBBIE: It was the year my friend had hardly any money, but she wanted to do some kind of holiday or adventure together with her kids. She wasn't a camper, but she read about these Tee Pees you could reserve in the Kananaskis country, and decided to rent one for the weekend. Even though she couldn't start a fire, didn't sleep a wink, and ended up taking the kids to McDonalds for breakfast, she lived the moment with what she had. Which remains one of her most treasured holidays.

Take a moment to think about people in your life. Who lives this legacy trait? It might be family, friends, an everyday encounter, a person from the past. Who lives now?

● TRAIT 7 REVIEW: Live Now

KEY CONCEPT

Embrace the moment. Whatever that looks like and however it feels, this moment is as it should be.

REALITY CHECK!

It is so easy to get caught up in dreaming of a future that doesn't yet exist, or worrying about what has happened in the past, that we completely forget about the time that we have in front of us right here and now. We know that this is a little bit of a contradiction because most of this book has been about planning for the future, defining your desired outcome, all that sort of thing. The irony is that the way to get there is to be here and live now. When you can do that, you are able to accept this moment, knowing it is as it should be, and at the same time, you can live now to make it become whatever you would like it to be.

Bring This Trait to Life

To make a difference, consider the following:

1. Right now, in this moment, where is my thinking?
2. Am I embracing this current moment as it is, feeling the here and now?
3. Where can this moment take me?

LEGACY

TRAIT 8:
Make Possible

KEY CONCEPT

Say yes to possibility. It is the embodiment of the "why not" attitude that breaks through to the most amazing wins.

Every one of us might find ourselves at times in a situation or circumstance that seems impossible. Obstacles can appear enormous, the pressure huge, the fear real. But the biggest thing holding us back is often ourselves. There are always ways through, even if they aren't apparent immediately. Think back on the times you made things possible for yourself. How did you do it? Think of all of the people who made things possible for you. What circumstance was created in order to make things possible to move ahead, to break through?

A Legendary Example of this Trait

Bill Gates *is an entrepreneur and philanthropist. Best known as one of the titans of the personal computer revolution, he made it possible for the technology that has advanced communication beyond our wildest imaginations. He has become a champion of numerous important causes. With his wife, Melinda, he has established the Bill and Melinda*

Gates Foundation. Following in the tradition of the Rockefellers and supported by Warren Buffet, he is donating large amounts of money to various charitable organizations and scientific research programs. Bill Gates is making opportunities possible for under-represented minorities, and for prevention of AIDS and prevalent diseases in third world countries.

Who do you know that shows this trait?

DEBBIE: It was at a colleague's funeral that I realized what this trait really meant. Working together with him, I knew of his anything-is-possible attitude. He worked with diving when they won gold at the Olympics, he worked with rowing when they became incredibly successful, he worked behind the scenes to make the Torino Olympic results the best ever. Hearing Olympic champion speakers from diving, rowing, and hockey share stories of his life, I saw he had influenced every single person or organization that he had worked with in a lasting and positive way.

Take a moment to think about people in your life. Who lives this legacy trait? It might be family, friends, an everyday encounter, a person from the past. Who makes possible?

LEGACY

● TRAIT 8 REVIEW: Make Possible

KEY CONCEPT
Say yes to possibility. It is the embodiment of the "why not" attitude that breaks through to the most amazing wins.

REALITY CHECK!
It is easy to focus on all of the things that we can't do, what might go wrong, what will work against us. With all of these ideas in our head, we stop ourselves before we even start. Making possible means staying open to the thousands and thousands of little things that we can do. It means remembering that embodying the "why not" attitude will ensure that some solution always presents itself, and makes possibilities appear for yourself and others.

Bring This Trait to Life
To make a difference, consider the following:
1. Are you able to find a way through, in spite of the challenges or odds against you?
2. If the circumstances aren't there to do what needs to be done, are you creating ones that will?
3. Are you championing the way of life that you want to see happen for yourself and others?

LEGACY

KEY CONCEPT SYNOPSIS
THE LEGACY TRAITS
Championing a Meaningful Way of Life

 Know yourself. Your values act as a compass, guiding your decision making, showing people who you are.

 Be kind. The way you respond, react, or simply are in situations can have an enormous impact on those around you.

 Break free from the status quo. Having the courage to challenge popular ideas often leads to breakthroughs and paves the way for others to follow.

 Appreciate diversity. We share common ground as human beings, and at the same time, we are all different and unique.

 Recognize your impact. Generously share your wisdom, knowledge, and experience with others.

 Embrace the moment. Whatever that looks like and however it feels, this moment is as it should be.

 Check your ego. Acknowledge contributions, admit mistakes freely, and shine the light on others.

Say yes to possibility. It is the embodiment of the "why not" attitude that breaks through to the most amazing wins.

LEGACY

LEGACY TRAITS—SELF ASSESSMENT

Before moving on in this book, take the time to think about how you bring each of the Legacy Traits to life. See what traits need more work than others and invest some time in them. This isn't about a rating scale. It is about awareness, and understanding how you bring each of the traits to life.

Legacy Trait

1. Embody Values

How do I bring this trait to life?

2. Challenge Convention

How do I bring this trait to life?

3. Influence Wisely

How do I bring this trait to life?

4. Have Humility

How do I bring this trait to life?

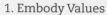
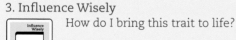

5. Show Goodwill

How do I bring this trait to life?

6. Celebrate Humanity

How do I bring this trait to life?

7. Live Now

How do I bring this trait to life?

8. Make Possible

How do I bring this trait to life?

LEGACY

CHAMPIONING THE GREAT TRAITS

We hope you have enjoyed the various perspectives that this book has presented throughout *The Champion's Journey* as much as we have enjoyed sharing them with you. We feel that our life's work—over seventy years combined of creating champions—is captured within these pages.

The first step of the journey was The Achiever Traits. Here, we outlined the fundamentals needed to connect you to your own win, achieving whatever you desire through the process. The next step was The Leader Traits. They outlined the fundamentals for creating winning results for the teams and organizations you are leading. The Legacy Traits closed the journey with the idea that no matter what you do, how you live your life will have a positive and meaningful impact—creating, truly, the lasting win.

Life is not about boxes and silos: It is much more fluid than that! The twenty-four Great Traits work like this, too. Sure, each seemingly stands alone, but at the same time, each trait works in conjunction with the others to make them stronger. The more the traits are used, the more dynamic they become—which is exactly what life calls for.

At any one time in your day, you might be an achiever, a leader, and a legacy leaver within the span of three minutes. You might be out doing something for yourself, you get a call from someone who needs you, and you interact with a stranger at a cash register. We are complex people living busy lives. The simplicity of the traits is, ironically, what allows them to adapt to the complexities of life. It is where the magic happens—when they *all* work together, coming to you as you need them!

By mastering all of the eight traits within the three sections of *The Great Traits of Champions*, the *right* traits start to come to mind, often in two's and three's and from different sections, when you most need them. Stay open to seeing what you need to be more aware of and what traits appear. They really work!

LEGACY

Remember, throughout this entire *Champion's Journey*, you determined the desired outcomes. As you keep using this book, keep defining those wins for yourself. Being a champion in the achiever sense means not settling for mediocrity and being the best at whatever you decide to do. Being a champion in the leader sense means creating an environment around you where excellence can thrive and great results can happen. Keep going for those winning results. Being a champion in the legacy sense means making a positive and meaningful impact. Continue to use your life for the lasting win.

We hope you have come to understand that it is ultimately the culmination of all three aspects of *The Champions' Journey* that creates YOUR legacy. You leave your legacy by what you achieve *and* how you lead others *and* who you are while doing it. That brings us to one last point of business. As you take ***The Great Traits of Champions*** out into the world, we want you to ask yourself one final question:

What kind of legacy are you leaving?

LEGACY

NOTES

NOTES

NOTES

NOTES